# THE
# SURVIVOR'S
# GUIDE TO
# UNEMPLOYMENT

## TOM MORTON

PIÑON PRESS

P.O. Box 35007, Colorado Springs, Colorado 80935

Library of Congress Catalog Card Number:
    92-64091
ISBN 08910-97015

Morton, Tom (G. Thomas)
    The survivor's guide to unemployment / Tom
Morton.
        p.    cm.
    Includes index.
    ISBN 0-89109-701-5 : $10.00
    1. Employees—United States—Dismissal of.
    2. Unemployment—United States—Psychologi-
cal aspects.    3. Unemployed—United States—Life
skills guides.    4. Job hunting—United States.
I. Title.
HD5708.55.U6M67    1992
650.14—dc20                           92-64091
                                          CIP

Printed in the United States of America

# Contents

*To all those wandering*
*through the wilderness of unemployment,*
*seeking a way home*

# Acknowledgments

This book would not have been possible without the encouragement and suggestions of many people, many of whom have felt the sting and confusion of joblessness. Chief among them is my sister, Paula, a Certified Financial Planner living in Cheyenne, Wyoming, who gave invaluable advice on personal money management. My parents, George and Marian Morton, and brother, Andrew, encouraged me not only with the book but through the duration of joblessness.

A heartfelt thanks goes to Bruce Nygren, Nancy Burke, Kathy Yanni, and the staff of Piñon Press for their guidance and patience.

Of the scores of unemployed persons who shared their experiences, I want to especially thank Julia, Lydia, Kathy, Melody, Charlie and Jorja, and Patrick and Jean.

Others who offered their advice include: Vicky Barber and Garth Lucero of the Consumer Protection Enforcement Section of the Colorado Attorney General's office; the current and formerly unemployed people on the Community News Service computer bulletin board in Colorado Springs; Dr. Foster Cline; Sue Davies and the Consumer Credit Counseling Service of Southern Colorado; Gretchen Decker of Manpower Temporary Services; Neil Duppen and those in the job-support group at Cherry Hills Community Church in Denver; Valerie Lorenz, executive director of the Compulsive Gambling Center in Baltimore; Don Peitersen of the Colorado Department of Labor and Employment; Henry Perritt, Jr., professor of law at Villanova University School of Law; Jon Talton of the *Rocky Mountain News* in Denver; and the Rev. Carol Wylie of Ecumenical Social Ministries of Colorado Springs.

Finally, the deepest gratitude goes to Rick and Sarah Ansorge, Andrea Jacobs, and Doug and Monica LeBlanc for their incomparable friendships.

# Introduction

Losing your job is one of the most stressful and painful events you can experience. Perhaps you'd been living under the threat of it for a long time, sensing the ominous gathering of storm clouds overhead. Or maybe it staggered you with a sudden blow, like a lightning strike out of the blue. Either way, you're out of work: another casualty from a personality clash, from a company's effort at "cost control," or from a national recession.

For some, unemployment will turn out to be a short-term nuisance that is quickly resolved. Not too long ago, that was the usual scenario. Most people who were fired or laid off could turn to other firms looking to hire. They stood a good chance of starting again at a salary close to—or even better than—what they were making before. Sure, they collected a few ego bruises along the way. But despite trimming a few expenses here and there, their lifestyle was basically unscathed. If they had previously been nervous about rumors of layoffs, perhaps they even experienced some relief that the pink slip had broken the haunting "what-if" tension over the future.

But since the recession that began in the summer of 1990, unemployment scenarios have taken a disturbing turn. Hiring freezes, early retirements, layoffs, and firings now cut across white- and blue-collar boundaries. And millions of people who have lost their jobs aren't technically "unemployed" according to the U.S. Bureau of Labor Statistics' official unemployment rate. They are underemployed—eking out a subsistence income on part-time jobs—or have become so discouraged that they've given up trying to find full-time work.

Families who traditionally relied on the paternal arm of a company, the military, or civil service now clutch empty air. The corporate arm has been yanked back, taking job security with it. Even the long-held taboo against layoffs before major holidays has been broken. And fear of job loss haunts millions who are still employed.

These changes in the unemployment scene have had drastic effects. People increasingly endure longer periods of unemployment. Jobs they've counted on for years are gone forever. Their self-esteem takes a nose-dive. They lose a sense of direction in life. They may even face the loss of family or home.

For many, losing a job means a permanent step away from the goal of a better life. Commentators even waggishly refer to ex-Yuppies (young, upwardly-mobile professionals) as "Dumpies" (downwardly mobile professionals). But it's not so funny if you're the one heading down.

We never took any courses in how to head *down* the job track. We didn't study the intricacies of filing for unemployment insurance benefits. We never took notes on how to collect charitable donations. Yet unemployment presents a unique set of challenges to coping with our finances, our self-esteem, our families, and our future. And so it requires a unique set of skills, talents, and new ways of thinking.

If you have the right tools for dealing with this period of transition, your unemployment can teach you important and valuable lessons that quite possibly will change the way you live for the rest of your life. But first you have to figure out how to survive the experience.

That's why *The Survivor's Guide to Unemployment* has been written: to help you through this time by giving you specific survival skills. This book is a manual on how to weather the initial crisis and cope with the basic stresses and issues accompanying unemployment.

What I offer arises from the practical advice of those in the business of helping the unemployed, along with the personal experiences of those who have lost their jobs and have struggled to find new lives— myself included. No two stories are identical, but they express common themes.

*The Survivor's Guide to Unemployment* is designed to help you think clearly about your experience of job loss. Its structure follows the pattern of events that usually happen when and after you lose your job. Some issues must be dealt with immediately. Others are clustered together and need sorting out. Still others can be put on hold temporarily. In the following pages, you'll find help and encouragement for mustering day-to-day survival skills as well as pursuing the long-term goal of finding a new job or career.

Although you'll find tips and a process for seeking new employment, this book does not duplicate the extensive advice available in scores of books, articles, and self-help guides for job hunting, résumé writing, and interviewing. Instead, the information here will help you put out the brushfires of your unemployment along the way so your job search can proceed effectively.

Even though unemployment is an intensely personal crisis, it's also a widespread one. You are not alone. Each month, hundreds of thousands of people like you sign up for unemployment insurance benefits. Thousands more try to cope without even that. All of us who have struggled through this excruciating experience have also struggled with the loneliness and self-doubt that go with it. As you read about what others have gone through and what they've learned in the process, I trust you'll gain perspective on your experiences and inspiration for your own future direction.

Unemployment is hard. It hurts. I wouldn't wish it on anyone. Yet it's taught me lessons about myself that no books or lectures could ever impart. I've grown personally. I've learned responsibility. I've seen how strong—and how weak—I really am. I've discovered that regardless of how joblessness happens, we're never quite the same again. We will change and be changed.

You have little control over the reality that you are unemployed. You have a great deal of control, however, over how you will handle it. With God's help, you can survive and even triumph.

The journey begins.

# I

❖

# "I've Never Felt So Scared"

—

# Coping with the Immediate Concerns

# CHAPTER ONE

# "I Thought I Was Somebody, Then I Lost My Job"

J anet had made it—or so she thought.

Years of night classes at the local community college taught her skills in personnel management and computer science. Hours of self-examination shook her out of the grind of $5.50-per-hour jobs and moved her to something better: human resources director for a small high-tech firm. Janet consistently garnered sterling performance reviews. She liked the hours, the status, the variety, and the money. And except for the company's arrogant president, she liked the people she worked with, too.

Janet's personal life began to level out. A decade earlier she had endured a bitter divorce, lost custody of her two children, and had to pay alimony. One child was now in college, so she had only one child to support. She began dating, too.

As part of this general upswing in her circumstances, Janet took control of her finances. She sold her house and moved into a modest apartment. She eliminated credit card debts and paid off her car. She wasn't rich, but she certainly wasn't poor either. She scrimped to put money into a vacation fund, finally fulfilling an eight-year dream to tour Europe.

Before she left for the vacation, however, the athletic forty-year-old noticed a nagging pain that shot up both arms. It seemed like the Carpal Tunnel Syndrome that some of her colleagues had developed from repetitive movements in using a computer keyboard. But visits to a physician yielded no diagnosis. She submitted the doctor bills through her company's insurance plan and caught the plane for Paris the next day.

Refreshed from her vacation, Janet returned to work. The company president called her into his conference room. "Miss Angstrom, your employment with our company is terminated as of today. The security guard will escort you to your office. There you will find boxes for packing your personal effects. We will mail you your last check."

"What—?" Janet gasped, trying to form a question before her throat parched.

"There is nothing to discuss, Miss Angstrom," the president curtly replied. He motioned the guard to Janet and walked out of the room.

The next half-hour swirled in a blur of tears, packing, and the puzzled faces of her coworkers. The security guard took her company identification card, pointed at the parking lot, and ordered her off the property. "The exit gate is that way," he said.

More tears, a lot of alcohol, and a week later, Janet began to recover from the shock. "I thought I was somebody, then I lost my job" is how she described it.

Initially, former coworkers called occasionally. But after a few weeks, the calls stopped coming. Rumors had been floating around the company about Janet's alleged poor performance and drug use. Senior management did nothing to quash the rumors. In fact, it was only too happy to fill in the sordid if untrue details.

The traumas of unemployment set in. Janet's pains in her arms intensified. Surgery helped little. The doctors ordered her not to look for work until they could identify and treat the problem.

Her worst experiences were trying to qualify for unemployment insurance and workers' compensation. Her former company blocked every move—with the help of a firm created expressly to maximize a company's profits by thwarting ex-employees from collecting benefits.

The money began to run out. Janet still owed child support, so she hired an attorney to delay payments. She cashed in savings bonds, but had to pay interest on them when she filed income tax the next year. She could qualify for assistance from the county's social services department only if she liquidated her retirement funds. She could do that without paying the penalties only if a doctor filed an affidavit stating that her health difficulties had lasted longer than a year.

Janet made ends meet through friends who bought groceries for her. She cashed in the aluminum cans and newspapers she found by her apartment's trash bins. Then her apartment manager told her that rent was going up 30 percent. Now she had to find a new place to live—but who would rent to someone without a source of income?

As Janet came to grips with the reality that she was destitute, she analyzed her situation and boiled the solutions down to plan A and plan B. Plan A consisted of a final appeal to get workers' compensation to pay for the surgeries and therapy, find a cheap apartment, and qualify for every food and clothing handout possible.

If those attempts failed, she would resort to plan B: suicide.

However, the thought of the devastating impact of plan B on her family and friends turned her back to the struggle for survival. One of her chief difficulties was regaining any sense of self-esteem. It began to return, gradually, as she located agencies to help with her daily needs, a job-support group sponsored through a local church, and a temporary job that required only minimal use of her arms. She longs for the day when she can work as a personnel director again.

Janet's story is a composite of several workers who lost their jobs for reasons known only to their bosses. (Their stories, like those recounted throughout this book, have had details altered to protect their identities.) But anyone who has lost a job knows that Janet's story rings true. The variations on it are played out in this country thousands of times each week.

## "I'VE NEVER FELT SO SCARED"

If you, a friend, or a family member have lost a job, you know that unemployment—or the fear of unemployment—is no longer a remote problem. It doesn't just happen to "the other guy." Now it's everybody's problem. It runs throughout society, with no respect for company loyalty, job performance, or socio-economic status.

Just because you studied, made sacrifices, and worked hard doesn't mean someone owes you a job. No sense of outrage or justice changes the hundreds of economic, technological, and social forces that have sent job security into extinction.

The shock to your system will reverberate in several areas. Joblessness will necessitate a severely curtailed personal or family budget. More painful than that, it possibly will mean that when you find work again it will not pay as well or provide the former benefits—even as you struggle to recoup the losses you experienced during unemployment.

Yet as hard as the economic crunch is, unemployment will severely test your personal and family relationships. You may have to move in with friends or family just to make ends meet. You may even need to move away from friends, family, and community to find employment. You will experience stress and grief as real as the loss of a loved one—maybe not as intense, but real nonetheless. The damage to your self-esteem and the resulting shame can translate into withdrawal or violence. The desperate search for solace can lead to the bottle, an affair, or even the barrel of a pistol. More marriages split up over financial difficulties than for any other reason. Unemployment exacerbates those tensions.

You may find that many relationships with people you worked with on a daily basis—even those you called dear friends—will fade and die. Many people won't know what to say to you or how to relate to you. Some will even insult you for the very fact that you are out of work, speaking with the prejudice that if you're out of work, you must be a bum. This is hard enough during a recession, but it's even worse during periods of economic growth.

Yet despite the financial and personal struggles and losses, you will need to do what it takes to find work again. For many, that's a matter of sending out hundreds of letters and résumés. And, if you're lucky, receiving just a smattering of responses. It may mean taking odd jobs—often part-time positions with no benefits—just to pay the bills.

However, the reverberations of the shock are not all bad. Unemployment can offer an opportunity to focus on what you really want. Hard economic times and the dizzying rate of technological change mean that you may need to reassess your career. It doesn't matter how well qualified you are for a job if it no longer exists.

Unemployment may also move you out of a job or career that you really didn't like anyway. You may need to retool your skills or reeducate yourself. This in turn could mean a further drain on your time, finances, and family. But you will reap the rewards by becoming self-empowered.

Finally, when you find work again—and you *will* find work again—you can apply the lessons of unemployment to your relationships, finances, and personal goals to gird yourself for the next possibility of finding a pink slip tucked in with your paycheck.

If you are employed, you might have a family member or friend who is going through unemployment. You need to know that you have power to hurt or heal. People out of work quickly find out who their friends are by their phone calls and generosity. You can do a great deal of good by lending a sympathetic ear, buying lunch, or treating your friend to a movie.

Please remember that unemployment is an intensely personal experience that's difficult to convey to others. For all my conversations and tears, one friend said she never really understood what was happening to me until it happened to her. She called one day to tell me that her boss was letting her go "because he says he can't afford me." Through her own tears she sobbed, "I've never felt so scared."

ARE YOU SCARED?

You may already be scared. Or you may have moved beyond fear to frustration and despair. Perhaps you're worried because you know something's up at work but you can't put your finger on it. That "something" could be the rumbling of impending layoffs or firings.

But the specter of losing your job or the trauma of unemployment doesn't mean that you have to be a passive victim. You can anticipate the possibility of job loss and then do something about it. You can let the shock to your system electrify you into action instead of numbing your ability to respond.

If you're currently employed but worried about your job, read through the next chapter for help in preparing for the possibility of finding yourself out of work. If you're already out of work, you may want to move on to chapter 3, which picks up at the "what do I do now?" stage—that first painful wave of finding out that the writing on the wall had your name on it.

# CHAPTER TWO

# "There's No Guarantees Anymore"— Anticipating Job Loss

❖

O n a steamy, late-summer day in 1984, Texaco U.S.A. announced that it would lay off 1,400 of its 3,000 employees at its Port Arthur refinery in southeast Texas. The early 1980s recession in the oil industry had already rocked the refinery, which had lost 2,000 employees in the previous twenty months. That same day, DuPont De Nemours E I & Co. announced it was closing a plant in nearby Beaumont, eliminating another 140 area jobs. But it was the Texaco announcement that really took everyone by surprise. My newspaper sent me to interview the workers and family members who might be affected.

In the aftermath, the lifelong loyalty of workers and their families gave way to uncertainty and despair. A few strapping pipe fitters cynically celebrated their first "layoff party" under a tree, listening to a van stereo and drinking beer. "When a baseball team messes up, they fire the managers, not the players," said one twelve-year employee. "We've all been here about ten to fifteen years. Most of us grew up together."

Another chimed in, "Texaco said we'd always have a job."

Yet another worker added, "About two months ago, [the plant manager] called us together and said there'd be no layoffs."

Seniority was worthless. Workers with fewer than twenty years with the company were sure that their days at the plant were numbered. One Port Arthur man—whose father was a thirty-two-year veteran of the refinery—said, "The American people have been flying on clouds [for years], but now the rest of the world is catching up. There's no guarantees anymore."

The grammar wasn't correct, but the sentiment certainly was. Years ago, blue-collar workers lost those guarantees of company loyalty to employees, union protection, and promises of lifetime jobs. But now, those guarantees are gone for everyone.

## THE NEW WORLD ORDER OF JOB INSECURITY

When America relied more on heavy industry to fuel the economy, blue-collar workers had something that few white-collar workers have now: a union safety net. Through the union, workers had a powerful ally in bargaining, a union hall for socializing and job hunting, strike funds, and pension funds. The possibility of at least temporary joblessness was a constant reality for those workers, and the union provided a means to get through the rough times of working life.

But white-collar employees who work in high technology, business, and service industries never really had that network. They tend to be more isolated from their peers than blue-collar workers are, and so many of them don't possess the skills to weather tough times. Education and professional status can't protect them from the fickle trends of the marketplace—whether the market is high tech, finance, communications, defense, foreign trade, transportation, or other industries. Even government jobs on the local, state, and federal levels—once thought to have ironclad security—are on the line.

In recent years, military personnel have discovered that there are no guarantees in promises of government employment in a "new world order." Especially since the collapse of the Soviet Union, they've had to relinquish their dreams of serving their country for twenty years, retiring, and then collecting their pensions.

As anyone who has ever lived in a "company town" can tell you, a layoff in the major industry will spread with a ripple effect to support companies and retail stores. These new breeds of potentially unemployed workers need ways to monitor what may happen to them in the workplace. They also need the means to be proactive in anticipating a layoff or other form of job loss.

## READING THE WRITING ON THE WALL

The more you watch for signs and signals, the more control you have over circumstances related to possible unemployment. You can't prevent a layoff, but you might be able to predict it by tracking your company's management, behavior, and performance. You may have more options in dealing with a personality conflict or impasse in which you find it intolerable to continue working where you are. And you have a great deal you can do to prevent the company for firing you for cause.

In this chapter we'll look at how to stay on the lookout for the possibility of unemployment. Even if you think your current job situation is fairly secure, you can still help yourself by cultivating these tips for greater vigilance. We'll look at three basic scenarios, aside from voluntary resignation, that can lead to losing your job: layoffs, resignations under duress, and firings for cause.

## LAYOFFS

American business has taken a meat-ax to the English language in recent years with its creative terms for describing layoffs: "downsizing," "downscaling," "streamlining," "cost-cutting," "reduction-in-force [RIF]," and my favorite, "surplussing." Perhaps business leaders reason that if the words are obscure enough, the pain or consequences for the workers or themselves will go away. They won't.

You won't be able to thwart a remote corporate decision to "surplus" employees, including yourself. But you don't have to be an innocent lamb led to the "streamlining" slaughter, either. You can play the way they do by monitoring the economy and your local company. When a company announces that it's laying off ten, a hundred, or a thousand workers, you can be sure that decision wasn't made overnight. It came after management spent months analyzing balance sheets and marketing trends.

### Reading Business Journals

If you're anticipating a layoff or firing, you can monitor the same things management watches—whether you work for General Motors or Mom's Pie Shop.

One of the primary channels for staying informed on market trends, the economy, and individual companies is the wide variety of business periodicals currently available at the newsstand or local library. You don't need an M.B.A. to understand them, either. *The Wall Street Journal, Business Week, Fortune, Forbes,* and *Barrons* are a few outstanding examples. Television and radio programs are also a good source of information, although they're not as detailed as what you'll find in periodicals.

Look for more than just strictly business news, however. Politics, too, affects business trends and decisions. Many publications, from local newspapers to magazines of all political persuasions, can improve your understanding of how federal, state, and local politics affect your profession or trade.

In addition to political trends, macroeconomic issues are another area to watch in order to stay alert for possible layoffs. We live in a global economy; national borders are increasingly irrelevant to how a company does business. For example, few automobiles are truly "American cars" anymore. Any given model can be designed in one country and assembled in another—with parts supplied from manufacturers all over the world. The global economy also affects where companies locate. Manufacturers will naturally look for operating sites where they can employ the least expensive labor, which in many cases may be overseas.

Macroeconomic factors ensure that layoffs, unemployment, new jobs in new fields, and corporate readjustments and realignments will be a permanent fact of life. Tracking business and technology trends through periodicals will help you stay abreast of developments in the global economy. This information may also come in handy for pursuing new career directions after a layoff. Recessions are painful, but in the long run they're healthy for the economy. They form a natural part of market forces. When recoveries pick up again, those who lost jobs during the slump must answer the question of what kinds of employment will now be opened up. If you've kept up on global business news, you stand a better chance of making wise choices about new career paths.

## Following Your Own Company and Industry
Another way to read the writing on the wall is to research business information about your employer. If your company is a publicly held firm, you can obtain analyses of your company's performance or goals to find out whether it's growing, on a plateau, or in decline. If your company is a privately held firm, information will be harder to come by, but you can still compare it with similar publicly held firms.

You may find, for example, that your company is planning to buy out another company or offer itself for sale. Such maneuvers are clear warning signs that layoffs may be around the corner, especially if both companies have workers doing similar jobs and the new, bigger company will need to cut excess employees. If the company doing the buying has to go deeply into debt to make the purchase, watch out. Massive debt will come back to haunt the new company.

Business periodicals can often tell you if your company is being sued or is under investigation by the government. Such actions could make upper-level managers skittish about undertaking new projects.

Extend your research beyond your particular employer to include your industry as well. Virtually all industries, from accounting to zoo-keeping, have their own professional journals. Any good public or university library will subscribe to them, particularly if they are related to local industries.

Information in these trade journals will be more technical than in the general business periodicals, but it can still give you a good idea of what's going on. You stand a better chance of getting straight reporting on what's happening in your own company from these periodicals than from your employer's in-house press releases.

Another fruitful source of information is corporate annual reports. They often provide the best analysis of what is happening, but you'll need to read critically in order to get that analysis. Keep in mind that the bad news of how your company is doing will be buried toward the back of the report, especially in sections comparing debt to equity ratios. Be wary of language warning, "No matter what you read in the press, Acme Inc. is doing just fine." Also watch for CorporateSpeak that puts a happy spin on unhappy trends and tough times, such as, "Despite depressed earnings and a shaky national economy, we foresee better times for Acme Inc."

Information on your company and industry is most likely more accessible (and easier to understand) than you might imagine. By reading and discussing what you find with your colleagues, you will become more informed—and therefore better able to make clear decisions about what to do if times get tough. If you think this is too much trouble to bother with, remember this: The people who make decisions about your job track the same trends and information.

### Reading the Writing on the Bulletin Board

A more informal way to gather information is simply by keeping your ear to the ground around the office. Many companies still use the old system of posting company news on bulletin boards. Astute employees, however, know that they can find the best news about their company at the coffee machine or water cooler (not on inter-office memos). Rumors remain one of the fastest forms of communication. They aren't always accurate and they usually don't convey the whole truth, but then neither do memos.

The following list of signs to watch for is based on the reflections of a number of unemployed or previously unemployed people who recalled that these circumstances preceded their layoffs. These incidents appeared innocuous at the time. In retrospect, however, they seemed significant as possible warning signals.

1. "The managers had a lot more meetings, and longer meetings, out of the office," observed one communications employee. "When they returned from their meetings, they put on a face of forced gaiety."
2. Promises of no layoffs, as the Texaco refinery workers discovered.
3. Promises of *no more* layoffs. Often the first layoffs aren't enough to solve a company's problems, as the Texaco refinery workers also discovered.
4. Drastic upper-management upheavals and/or shuffling of middle-management positions ordered by corporate headquarters.
5. Increasing frequency of divide-and-conquer management tactics by unscrupulous bosses to pit employees against each other.
6. Proposed layoffs of subordinates in which you, a supervisor, are asked to coordinate or serve as the designated hit-man (or hit-woman). Your supervisors may have designs on you, as you and they have designs on your subordinates.
7. The nearing of the completion of a project, with no other projects under proposal.
8. Frequent appearances by outside consultants and "experts" wandering through the premises. (They may have been hired to trim the organizational fat.)
9. Increased verbal abuse or angry looks from your bosses.
10. Overt or covert pressure to quit.
11. Tensions between supervisors and the company owners.
12. Fewer perks, such as the cancellation of Christmas bonuses and company picnics.
13. Cost-cutting measures that affect the way you do business, such as supervisors' demands for fewer business lunches or

penny-pinching in restocking supplies.
14. Positions remaining unfilled after employees leave.
15. Unattainable goals set by supervisors.
16. Revisions of benefit plans, to employees' disadvantage.
17. Functions or accounts traditionally handled by your office are transferred to other offices.
18. Company morale steadily deteriorates.

## RESIGNATIONS UNDER DURESS AND FIRINGS WITHOUT CAUSE

In addition to layoffs, a second major area to watch out for is forced resignations. Usually, resignations under duress are focused on a single employee or a small group of employees.

Management reasons here may be due to industry or macroeconomic factors, such as those we looked at above. In this case, management targets an individual or group who are perceived to be no longer necessary to company goals. Instead of a company-wide layoff, they ask for resignations. Sometimes, however, the forced resignation or firing without cause begins and ends with a personality clash.

For maintaining good references in future job searches, a forced resignation because of circumstances beyond your control will look better on a résumé than a firing. However, it can cut the other way by disqualifying you for unemployment insurance benefits if the official version is that you left the company voluntarily.

### Contractual Issues

In recent years, companies have increasingly written "employment-at-will" clauses into their employer-employee contracts. These clauses make it easier than ever before for companies to request resignations from their employees. These clauses provide a legal agreement that either employer or employee may part company at any time, *for any reason*. That gives you leeway to leave whenever you want. But it also gives the company a powerful legal weapon for saying to you, "Here's your check—clean out your desk, and don't let the door slam when you walk out."

### Contract Buyouts

If you have had a contract with a firm, and the firm needs to reduce its workforce, it may offer to buy out your contract. This kind of resignation, however painful, is often a good arrangement because it leaves your résumé and references intact for future job prospects. A buyout often includes a hefty severance and benefits package. Although it may disqualify you for unemployment insurance benefits, at least for a while, it could far exceed anything your would receive from the state department of labor and employment.

## Personality Clashes

Even when contract buyouts are unhappy partings, however, they still can't compare to the anguish when you and your boss are locked in a bitter personality dispute. Those disputes may range from disagreements over how both of you believe a job should be done, to sex discrimination or racism, to vehement dislikes over dress or attitudes.

Personality conflicts at work are among the ugliest of human relations. They often mask more deeply rooted issues of how you perceive each other personally and professionally. A personality conflict will make your life miserable. It's a fact of life that some people just don't like other people. And some people vent their own internal conflicts by treating others poorly.

When personality conflicts come to a head, such serious issues as racism, sex or age discrimination, or sexual harassment probably will give you legal grounds to fight the resignation in court. You will need to consult a lawyer about these issues.

## Impasses

There are times when you and your employer have such profound disagreements about how you should do your job that the situation deadlocks at an impasse. Since they write the checks, they win and you lose.

This happened to me. As a reporter for a city newspaper, I had a long-running debate with management over how the paper should deal with my beat. Tensions mounted and personalities clashed. As depression set in, my writing disintegrated.

After more than a year of agitating for change, I snapped. I told one of my editors of my intention to leave the paper, though it wasn't my intention to quit until I found another job. He said he wouldn't argue against my decision. Two days later, he said we were at an impasse, and I was effectively fired. His supervisors had told him to tell me that I would soon be gone. Ultimately, my dismissal was recorded with the personnel office as a resignation at his request.

In many cases management will resolve an impasse by making life so miserable for you that the only way to resolve it is to resign.

Karen worked as a broker in the mid-eighties for a company that contracted for work through a now-defunct savings and loan. Despite her impressive sales record, however, she couldn't coax a straight answer from her supervisors when she requested a promotion. Management turned a project of hers over to a colleague. It then demoted her without telling her.

Karen's health deteriorated from the pressure, and she developed an ulcer that nearly hospitalized her. "I started looking, thought that maybe something would change, and kept holding out that hope," she said. Nothing changed.

Karen's boss then told her that he was effectively cutting her pay by 50 percent. A week later, she submitted her two-week notice. Her ulcer began healing literally overnight.

"Sometimes the only thing you can do is quit," she said, recalling what a management consultant once told her. "You're out there with a weight around your neck, and you reach the point where all you can do is walk away."

Karen's situation brings up the issue of health factors. Companies practice a wide range of policies over debilitating health problems that affect work performance. Some are very generous and will provide ample time off for recuperation. Others are downright cruel and will dictate firing or forced resignation, even if it means the employee will lose health or pension benefits.

FIRINGS FOR CAUSE

Not all job losses stem from macroeconomic issues, corporate takeovers or failures, or temperamental bosses. Sometimes people don't do what they're supposed to do, do an inferior job of it, or cause trouble for others on the job. If they don't improve, even after repeated counseling and warnings, supervisors may conclude that the only recourse is to cut them loose.

Supervisors also may dismiss an employee for misconduct on the job, such as fighting or intoxication. An employer may even fire an employee for misconduct off the job if the employer can legally prove that the employee's misconduct damaged the employer's business.

The trials of unemployment may be the same for those who are laid off or fired without cause, but those who are fired for cause will need to deal with their own responsibilities about *why* they lost their jobs. They can't blame others for their own shortcomings, and will need to resolve those problems or else run the risk of getting fired for cause again.

## ALLAYING THE FEARS OF JOB LOSS

It's a jungle out there—even though the jungle is a modern office building with carpeting, computers, fax machines, desks, and telephones. Let's assume that you and your coworkers have heard rumors of layoffs, read accounts of upper-management squabbles, and figured out that the bottom line in the annual reports sank into the company's river of red ink. Now what do you do?

You don't need to face your future passively. You have two ways to see the jungle for the trees: a public way through your relationships at work, and a private way by keeping records.

### Build Relationships

The easiest way to face what's happening is to do it with others. Adopt the attitude, "We're all in this jungle together." You can derive more support from your colleagues than you might think. They can provide useful tips about what is happening, ideas about where to begin a job search, or just a shoulder to cry on. As much as possible, stay on good social terms with your coworkers—whether through parties, on coffee breaks or at lunch, or in ball games after work.

This solidarity has its Achilles heel, however. Confidants may try to turn inside information to their own advantage—especially if they want your job. Be vigilant for these unscrupulous predators, especially if your supervisors are known for fostering dissension among employees.

### Keep Records

Whether you feel paranoia about a possible layoff or uneasy about a growing personality conflict between you and your supervisor, it's very important that you keep records *at home*. At the least, they will give you a battery of documents to study so you're able to explain the situation clearly when you start interviewing for another job. But more importantly, they will give you valuable ammunition if you need to take legal action or appeal a denial of unemployment insurance benefits.

*These steps and precautions in no way imply that you should steal company property or violate company policies.* There are plenty of ways you can look out for yourself without risking an illegal act that could get you fired for cause and even prosecuted.

Where do you start? First, at least once or twice a year, compare what you actually do on the job with your job description, and review your personnel file. If you were told you would have an annual or semi-annual performance review, you have every right to expect management to carry out that responsibility. These job descriptions, performance reviews, and related documents should be written down and kept on file, and you should be permitted to keep your own copies.

Second, keep a diary. In addition to tracking your daily or weekly tasks, include the following:

1. Puzzling comments that seem innocuous at the time.
2. Notes about personnel changes.
3. Increased frequency of managers' meetings.
4. Strained conversations and/or sharp words between you and supervisors.
5. Comments conveyed to you by immediate supervisors about what *their* supervisors say about you.
6. Rumors.
7. Observations about whether your supervisors can look you in the eye and talk straight to you.
8. Any incidence of supervisors or others entering your computer files.
9. Minutes from meetings with supervisors, especially those in which you have disagreements.
10. Racist or sexist comments, derogatory remarks about age, disabilities or religion, and incidents of sexual harassment. Note management's reactions when you complain.
11. Reactions to your suggestions.
12. Notes about your health. If you get ill or need surgery, chronicle events and stipulate whether the illness was work-related.

A diary should include more than just grim comments, however. If your performance is complimented, write it down. Then if groundless criticisms arise later, you can refer back to the compliments.

In addition to keeping your own personnel record and maintaining a diary, file these other forms of documentation at home:

1. All pay stubs.
2. Copies of projects for your portfolio.
3. Your job description.
4. A duplicate file of your clients and contacts.
5. Copies of performance reviews.
6. Copies of newspaper or magazine stories about how your company is doing.

Remember that real or perceived paranoia about unemployment is no excuse to slack off. Strive to develop a pleasant attitude at work, even if it's tough. Practice initiative with projects. Do the best job you can, and don't allow corporate upheavals to infect you with the attitude, "If they don't care about me, why should I care about performing for them?" A good effort from you and your coworkers may be the crucial factor in a corporate decision to keep your division, delay a layoff, or allow you to transfer.

## NOW WHAT?

You've learned to track your company's performance as well as the ebb and flow of the economy. You've kept a sharp ear out for the rumors, and a sharper eye for changes in the office or shop. And you've maintained files at home about your performance.

You are becoming self-empowered. You are training yourself to be less a victim of the vagaries of Wall Street or the whims of managers, and more a proactive person in charge of your future. The knowledge you gain could prove very valuable if you are called on the carpet to defend yourself and give reasons why you should continue working for the company. What you learn might even be enough to persuade you to start looking for another job.

Will self-empowerment prevent a layoff or a forced resignation? Sadly, no. As the Texaco refinery workers knew, most companies aren't run like baseball teams. When the corporate club slides to the bottom of the league, the players go before the managers do.

So despite your best efforts and professional vigilance, you may be called out next. Suddenly you find yourself with free agent status. What then?

# CHAPTER THREE

# When You Get the Word

◆◆

"Y ou're fired."

"We're letting you go."

"The plant is shutting down in two months."

The actual notice of a firing or layoff will whack you in the stomach with the force of a baseball bat. People say that they felt weak, nauseated, dizzy, and even convulsed with pain. Others have said that when they get the word, they feel nothing—the words sound as if they're traveling through a pipe.

Variations on getting the word center around the same two basic themes: sudden and anticipated. Neither one is necessarily easier or harder to handle than the other. A sudden notice will certainly stun you, but it has the small benefit of getting you through the shock quickly. With many such notices, the dismissal means that you're gone that day. A sudden notice, however, also means that you have less reaction time for the other events immediately following.

An anticipated firing or layoff culminates the period of waiting and speculation. You may feel relief that the suspense or tension building up over weeks, months, or even years has finally been broken. You no longer have to put up with the unpleasant surprises, the personality conflicts, the hassles of uncertainties. Now you know it's over.

This kind of relief is similar to what families feel when a dying loved one finally or suddenly succumbs. Despite the tragic dimension, there is the very real belief and healthy reaction that the immediate level of suffering is over. Once the pain breaks open and the fear reaches an endpoint, the grieving process can begin.

Dana worked for a subcontractor at a plant that required tight government security. His supervisor had committed an infraction with Dana's help, and told Dana to lie if the plant investigators asked what he knew about the incident. Dana initially did as he was told, but on subsequent questioning confessed to his minor role in the incident.

Dana was sent home. He waited for two weeks before hearing about his fate. Then the news came: the subcontracting firm needed a scapegoat, and he was it. "After the two-week game, I was mentally prepared," Dana said. "When they let me know, it lifted a burden and I could get on with my life."

## HOW TO REACT
### The New Early Warning System
In 1988, employees threatened by layoffs or firings gained an ally with The Worker Adjustment and Retraining Notification (WARN) Act. According to the *Labor Relations Reporter* (Bureau of National Affairs, Inc.), this legislation requires employers with one hundred or more employees to give sixty days' advance notice of (1) shutdowns affecting at least fifty workers and (2) layoffs lasting more than six months and affecting one-third of the workers at the site.

The intent of this law is to give workers time to prepare for the job loss. This notification doesn't make unemployment easier as such, but the lead time helps workers think more clearly about what to do.

### Taking Control
You may not have the meager benefit of advanced notice. In any case, however, whether you alone get fired or you're laid off along with hundreds of coworkers, it's in your best interest to follow this important rule of reaction: *Control your emotions*. Get control of yourself instead of letting others control you. How you handle subsequent developments depends largely on how well you can pull this off.

Any harsh verbal or physical reaction on your part quite probably would be used to dismiss you on the spot. You could then be fired for cause, which would return to haunt you with difficulties with references, filing for unemployment insurance benefits, and applying for jobs. If you feel that your reaction will be too overwhelming—whether by swearing or another strong verbal response, an urge to slug your boss, or even just breaking down and crying—simply leave the room.

For the most part, it will be almost as uncomfortable for your supervisor to fire you as it is for you to hear it. (Of course, your supervisor will get over it a lot sooner than you will.) You may very well experience shock. You will have difficulty catching your breath, not to mention forming coherent thoughts. But you need to control yourself for the moment to sort out several issues.

First, it's important to act as professionally as possible. Acting professionally means you carry yourself and conduct yourself in a conservative and dignified manner. Don't be cute. Don't be sarcastic. Give straight answers to their questions, just as you want them to provide straight answers to yours. If your supervisors are obstinate or unwilling to talk, at least you know that you have done the best you can.

Acting professionally means that you'll need to act stoically. Getting the word about a job dismissal will hurt badly, and that hurt will show in your face. But if you can sit on some of that pain at least until you get home that night, do so.

It helps to have a friend spend some time with you after work to talk it over. If your friends are really friends, they will be able to roll with the punches of your anger. But as we discussed in the last chapter, be careful who you talk to. Real friends can help you think clearly and handle your emotions. Unscrupulous coworkers can take your pain and use it for their own ends. This is especially important if your actual termination date is still a few weeks or months away.

Second, in addition to reacting professionally, refrain from saying anything that could harm discussions about severance packages or future references. Don't give your supervisors any more ammunition to treat you poorly than they already have. Watch what you say. Depending on whether state laws allow it, you may be tape-recorded. Say nothing that could incriminate you.

Third, as best as you can, make your supervisor state explicitly *what* is happening. Make him or her state explicitly *why* this is happening. This is uncomfortable for you, and it probably is uncomfortable for your supervisor. You can turn this discomfort to your advantage, even though it will feel awkward to do so. Employers are not obligated to tell you what is happening or why they're firing you. But in the heat of the moment you might be able to get information from them that they wouldn't part with later on when they feel more in control.

Fourth, if your supervisor asks you to sign a statement promising that you will not take legal action, *don't sign it!* Your company may even throw in a cash incentive of an extra week's pay or more. Turn it down. Even though you will need the money, you will also need the leverage of legal option. Waivers aren't always ironclad, but signing one makes it tougher if you later think you should take legal action. Make it your goal to stay in charge as much as possible throughout the awful process of losing your job—no matter how out of control you feel.

## SHOULD YOU HIRE AN ATTORNEY AND SUE?

Refusal to sign a "no sue" clause doesn't mean that you *should* turn around and sue your company, however. We're a litigious society. Our answer to far too many problems is "sue the bums." But that doesn't mean you should just give up, either.

The advice not to sign a waiver, as well as much of the information in the rest of this section, comes from Henry H. Perritt, Jr., a professor at Villanova University School of Law. Perritt wrote the authoritative *Employee Dismissal Law and Practice* (published by Wiley Law Publications, John Wiley & Sons, Inc.). He also served as deputy undersecretary of labor in President Gerald Ford's administration. The following advice on whether to sue a former employer comes from his years of study and his counsel to employees, employers, and unions.

Your most basic issue as a new ex-employee, according to Perritt, is deciding in a fairly narrow window of time whether to sue or forget about it. You must make this decision within sixty to ninety days of your dismissal, because the validity of your case weakens every day.

You also must reckon with the likelihood that a lawsuit will take over your life, and consequently hurt your reputation in the labor market. A prospective employer will think twice about you upon discovering that you are taking your last employer to court. "If this person is doing this to his last boss," the reasoning goes, "what will he do to *me*?"

Your age and experience are also critical factors in whether to sue and how strong your case will be. If you are relatively young, lack a substantial history in the job market, and have a weak legal case, it's probably unwise for you to seek legal recourse. On the other hand, if you're older and have a lot of experience, you may have less to lose in the labor market. In that case, it may be worth your while to sue a former employer.

Perritt cites your geographical location as another factor to consider. Each state has its own body of law about wrongful dismissal.

For example, if you live in Georgia, Louisiana, or Florida, your chances for winning a wrongful dismissal suit are low. If you live in Montana, however, the likelihood is good that you might win.

You also must come to grips with the traditional "employment-at-will" rule. This means that employers start with the power to fire an employee at any time for any reason or no reason. However, several legal doctrines and scores of federal and state statutes since the early 1970s have weakened this rule. As a dismissed employee, your legal task is to show that you are entitled to some exception to the employment-at-will rule. Although the legal fine-tuning is evolving, the basic theories about employee dismissal law are constant, according to Perritt.

Perritt identifies six basic grounds on which employees may sue:

1. *Discrimination.* This includes any form of discrimination that is prohibited by statute law: race, sex (and pregnancy), age, disability, national origin, and religion. To prove this, you need to be able to show that a coworker who was like you in every way except for one characteristic was treated more favorably than you by a supervisor because of that one characteristic.

2. *An implied contractual right.* In most states, you can establish that you had contractual rights implied in highly specific provisions in personnel policies and employee handbooks. For example, let's say your employee handbook stated that nobody would be dismissed without good cause, or only after a warning or review by the chief personnel officer. If you were fired without warning or review, that may be grounds for filing suit.

Another strong legal case based on contracts occurs if you quit your job to go to work for an employer based on that employer's promise of job security, and the employer subsequently fires you. But you must be able to establish clearly that a legitimate promise of job security was made. Vague comments to you, such as "we're all one happy family here," are shaky ground on which to sue over a violated contract.

3. *Public policy tort.* You may have a case if you were fired after some kind of whistleblowing (such as reporting pollution to the proper authorities) or some other legally privileged conduct, such as serving on a jury or refusing to take a polygraph test. In many states, but not all, if you were dismissed and can establish that you engaged in that kind of legally privileged conduct, you can recover under what is known as public policy tort theory.

4. *Statutory whistleblowing.* You may have another kind of case if

you were fired for whistleblowing. Whistleblowing may be protected under a statute like the Clean Water Act. However, if you were a marginal worker, your case for legal action in this context may be weak.

5. *Defamation*. If there is unusual conduct surrounding the discharge, such as a supervisor denouncing somebody in front of a group of employees or lying about someone to prospective employers, that might give rise to a tort claim such as defamation. These charges are different from the discharge itself.

6. *Public employees*. If you are an employee of a governmental entity such as a school board or state or local government, you may be able to appeal to some constitutional claims. However, these claims are available only to employees in the public sector.

Finally, and perhaps most importantly, remember that each situation of employee dismissal is unique. The circumstances may not be unique, but you are. The only way you can be sure that you may have a case is to consult an attorney. Henry Perritt points out that many people don't realize they can buy a lot of legal advice for fifty to a hundred dollars. In many cases, depending on the state and the policies of the state bar, the initial consultation is free.

## NEGOTIATING FOR SEVERANCE PAY AND BENEFITS

In some companies, negotiating for severance is not even an issue. If a plant is shutting down that day or week, you'll be fortunate to get out with your shirt and lunch box. If you work in a small business, chances are there simply won't be enough money.

For the most part, you are at the mercy of your about-to-be ex-employer. Many companies prorate severance packages based on the length of time a laid-off employee spent with the company. Many companies also offer job placement services along with monetary severance. Or they might simply avoid the subject, expecting you to do the same. You should still ask, though. You can show your supervisor that you are in charge of your emotions, and that you expect him or her to act on your fair request.

If you're a middle manager, you should try to find what those in similar professions have been able to gain in severance when they lost their jobs. You also should contact former employees of the company and ask them if and what sort of arrangement they made in negotiating a severance package. You can then apply that knowledge to your severance negotiations.

Remember that if you do receive severance, the state agency in charge of distributing unemployment insurance benefits considers it earned income, just as it does with vacation pay or commissions received after you quit working. You must report any severance to the state when you file for unemployment insurance benefits.

## THE EXIT INTERVIEW

Many companies conduct exit interviews of their employees, regardless of the circumstances of their departures. Ideally, an exit interview can give a company a glimpse of what an employee really thinks. That in turn could affect how the company makes plans for the future. (Of course, the company may not care at all, either.)

Responding truthfully and rationally to an exit interview won't necessarily help your situation, but it may spark changes in the company's future. The exit interview will give you an opportunity to show your bosses and personnel director how strong you are. Be sure to find out exactly what benefits you are entitled to, *and get them in writing*.

If your company conducts exit interviews, take advantage of them. In advance of the interview, request that your personnel director give you the questions that will be asked of you, and then study them and write out your answers beforehand. Scheduling an exit interview implies that you will have some time to prepare. Don't blow off the interview as a cynical attempt at "sensitivity" by the company. Even if it really is cynical, you still owe it to yourself to behave with dignity.

Use the exit interview as a way to state your case for the last time. Spell out what your job description was, how you understood it, and the chronology of what happened leading up to your dismissal. If the interview is conducted orally, take notes. Better yet, tape it. Be truthful, factual, and concise. Don't embellish your story or get emotional.

This is the time to clarify what, if any, benefits you have coming. For example:

☞ Vacation pay, sick pay, and any other paid leaves you haven't taken.
☞ Any overtime.
☞ Severance package, including whether it will be distributed in a lump sum or over several weeks or months, and what, if any, job placement programs the company offers.
☞ Pension plans.

☞ Insurance plans.

☞ 401-K and other retirement plans.

☞ The summary plan description of medical insurance.

Request that the exit interview be entered as a permanent record in your personnel file, and keep a copy for yourself. Ask the personnel director for a copy of management's response to the content of your interview. If the management does not respond to your exit interview after a month, note that in your calendar or personal journal.

If you are asked to explain to a prospective employer why you left or were dismissed from your previous job, you already have rehearsed the answer in your exit interview. And if your former employer didn't respond to your exit interview, you may want to mention that. The lack of response may not be a tacit admission that you were right, but it does show that your ex-employer wasn't willing to state that you were wrong.

## RESPONDING TO RUMORS

When people are talking about you, there's not much you can do about it. One friend who was at her desk, summoned to a conference room, fired, and out on the street in an hour recalls, "What was so bizarre was how fast the news traveled. How did the word get around that fast?"

Rumors will fly around your office about why you are leaving or why you left. In keeping with the nature of gossip, rumors fuel speculation, which in turn fuels more rumors, and so on. If you've had good friends and supportive colleagues, you can reasonably expect that the rumors will be kept to a minimum. But sometimes it's to the advantage of management to let damaging rumors about you circulate through the office or shop. Those rumors can serve to keep a workplace divided and fearful, which may shore up management's power.

You can't do much about what people say about you, but you can control how you will react to the rumors. Keeping your dignity in the office for your remaining time, whether it's an hour or a month, will help snuff out many of the rumor brushfires. *You* know best why you are leaving or why you left. If you've had the opportunity to lay out your case in your exit interview, or calmly tell your coworkers what happened, you can do little else. Excessive efforts at rumor damage control on your part will only fuel suspicion about what happened.

Rumors can become serious problems, however, when prospective employers call former supervisors or coworkers for references. A nega-tive comment on the part of a supervisor, or even a well-nuanced pause when he or she is asked about you, can be enough to torpedo your chances at a new job. However, you do have a powerful legal ally. Ex-employees have successfully sued their former companies for badmouthing them on the grounds of interference with business. Many companies recognize that they're on very shaky ground when their management criticizes a former employee. These firms have poli-cies that only the personnel director is allowed to comment on a former employee, and the only information they supply is date of employment, date of departure, and salary history.

You can take comfort in the recognition that rumors about you, whether favorable or unfavorable, will fade over time. As memories dwindle, people will close ranks and eventually close their mouths.

SAYING GOODBYE

For the most part, your actual departure will be hard. You may have as little time as an hour or as much as a few months. There are two major considerations when the time comes: emotional and practical.

**Emotional Considerations**

If you are fired or laid off outright, the pain could be intense. If you are ordered to be gone that day, you will have to compress a lot of emotions and thoughts into a small amount of time. Remember to act professionally and control your anger. There will be time enough later for emotional download. You may not feel like saying goodbye even to your close coworkers. Don't worry about it. You can do that later.

If you receive notice of termination and have a week or longer, you are in a better position to put your best face forward. You will have the opportunity to spend time with your coworkers, contact clients, and take an exit interview.

Even though the departure will be hard, you can prove to others just how strong you are. Act professionally, smile even when it hurts, shake hands, and look everyone in the eye. If your supervisors act insecurely and avoid you, that's their problem.

**Practical Considerations**

Controlling your emotions after a sudden firing or layoff is important for a much more practical reason than simply avoiding an ugly scene.

You need to keep a clear head in order to be sure that you retrieve all your personal and business effects.

Collect all business cards, client lists, books, notes, and whatever else belongs to you—especially if it's potentially useful for networking or future business opportunities. Print out what files you can from your computer. It's not uncommon, however, for supervisors to bar your access to your computer files.

If you have only an hour to clean our your desk and files, and especially if management has assigned a security guard to watch your every move, just stash everything in a box. You can sort it out later. When you pack, don't make comments, sarcastic or otherwise.

*This advice is not to be construed as license to steal from your company.* On the other hand, don't let a firing become an opportunity for your company to confiscate what you have worked hard to build.

If you have been given even as little as a day to clear out, be methodical. Access files and client lists, and assemble them in an orderly manner. If you have time, inform your customers and clients, and get a running start on networking. When you contact them, refrain from emotional outbursts. It's probably best to avoid saying that you were fired. Work on an explanation that you and the company had a parting of the ways, and you hope the clients, customers, and sources will be doing business with you in the future.

## MAKING A GRACEFUL EXIT

Walking out of the plant, the shop, or the office for the last time may be one of the rare opportunities in your life for behaving with grace and dignity in the face of an excruciatingly difficult circumstance. Even if you have no job prospects, hold your head up, smile, and walk tall.

Don't get me wrong—this isn't easy. You can cry later, and you probably will. As you close out this phase of your career, you enter the statistical realm of the unemployed. You may be treated like a number, and you may feel a lot worse later on. But you can at least embark on what might be the beginning of a long dry spell of unemployment by proving to yourself and your coworkers what you're really made of. And if there's a family waiting for you when you return home, you will want to support them even as you will need all the support they can give you in the uncertain future that's now beginning.

# CHAPTER FOUR

# What to Tell Your Family

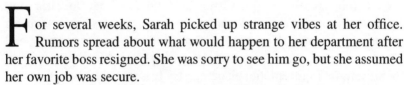

For several weeks, Sarah picked up strange vibes at her office. Rumors spread about what would happen to her department after her favorite boss resigned. She was sorry to see him go, but she assumed her own job was secure.

One day at 4:10 p.m., her new supervisor beckoned, "Would you come into my office, Sarah?" The dismissal was over in two minutes. She packed her things and was gone by 5:30.

On the way home, she stopped by a friend's house, talked for several hours, and asked him to follow her home. Sarah—a single mom in her early forties—could handle the shock, but she wasn't sure about her son. That's why she asked Bill to help.

When she and Bill came home, she looked her seventeen-year-old straight in the eye and said, "Bob, I lost my job today."

Bob, whose father had walked out of his life when he was two, went ballistic. "Mom! They can't do this to you! You've worked there for fifteen years. What are we going to do? We're going to lose the house!"

That's when Bill covered for Sarah. "Bob," he replied calmly, "they can do this to your mom, and they did. Your mom will need your support like never before."

## BREADWINNERS AND BREAD-EATERS

Unemployment can tear a family apart or pull it together in surprising ways. Much of that depends on how well the family supports the member who has lost his or her job. It also depends on how well the unemployed person can accept that support, no matter how much or how little it is.

Newly unemployed family members often stare down a double-barreled dilemma: the very people they need the most are often the very people their unemployment may hurt the most. A truthful but loving announcement of the new condition can go far in preparing family members for what is to come.

This chapter is designed to help you with the immediate issues surrounding breaking the news of job loss to your family. Details on surviving financially and in other ways will be dealt with in later chapters. Since each family has unique relational and financial considerations, you will need to tailor the following suggestions to your family circumstances.

## THE SHAME OF IT

Breaking the unemployment news to family members has never been easy. But because of economic upheaval in recent years, losing a job is not an unusual occurrence. Chronic unemployment throughout nearly all lines of work has become more common, which in some cases tempers the stigma of joblessness.

Most parents of the seventy-seven million children born in the so-called Baby Boom era (1946 to 1964) endured at least some of the Great Depression and much of World War II. They also benefited from the dramatic post-war economic growth. Although before World War II Americans were familiar with the hardship of losing a job, during the war and into the next two decades Americans became accustomed to the widespread availability of steady work. Companies and unions fostered institutional loyalty. Unemployment was usually a temporary problem or the result of a strike or lock-out, but the underlying assumption of such events was that full employment—often with one firm for life—was the norm.

The work ethic was stronger then than it is now. The benefit of a strong work ethic, of course, was that labor was valued and productivity was the result. One liability of such an ethic, however, was that it denigrated those who were out of work. People who were chronically unemployed were regarded as unstable, if not flawed in character.

Consequently, it was common during that era to view unemployment, or even serious difficulty at work, as not just an economic difficulty, but a cause for personal shame. Our parents' and grandparents' generation had learned during the Great Depression that a person hung on to his job and didn't talk about his problems. Life was tough enough without having to burden others, especially when the problem was unemployment.

My father—who went to work for a living at age ten during the Depression—was a lifetime employee for a major defense firm. In the early seventies he encountered a severe personality conflict at work. His job was on the line for more than a month. But at home, he wasn't talking. We kids knew something was wrong, but we didn't know what it was. I was attending college at the time, and I said some very insensitive things to my parents about the tension in the family. But my father never told me what really happened to him until I lost my job nearly two decades later. By then, the memories had softened and the stigma had disappeared.

The silence and shame over possible or actual job loss have been tempered by the times. As business and labor have adapted to the new global economy, the corporation and the union are no longer the bulwarks of stability they once were. Job loss has become a common phenomenon. This doesn't make unemployment any easier to live through. But jobless individuals are less likely today to be stigmatized with personal shame, because lots of people are experiencing the same thing.

You already know that losing your job is tough. But you also know that most people will be more tolerant of your situation than they would have been several decades ago. So it's reasonable to expect that your family will be more tolerant, too. You might find wellsprings of support that you never imagined as you break the news to your parents, spouse or spouse-to-be, boyfriend or girlfriend, or children.

## WHAT TO TELL YOUR PARENTS
Most parents try to raise their children to become self-sufficient, productive citizens. If you're out of a job, you might feel that you've somehow let them down. You may wonder how they will handle the news, and whether they will experience a sense of failure because of it. In any case, you will probably feel awkward about telling them.

Much of what you say and how your parents react depends on how strong your relationship is. If you've had supportive parents, you probably will be able to tell them shortly after you've received the notice of your dismissal. If they remember the Great Depression, they have firsthand memories of hardship, regardless of how much they profited from the post-war boom. Possibly they have experienced unemployment themselves. They are also likely to be more informed about what is going on in the economy than most people your age. All these factors can translate into a strong base of support, possibly with offers of financial or other assistance.

If your relationship with your parents hasn't been so strong, however, you may want to delay telling them. Sarah, the woman who was summarily dismissed by her new supervisor, had endured years of nagging from her mother about how Sarah couldn't really care for herself or her children without a man's help. So Sarah waited ten days before calling with the bad news. "I let one weekend pass before I did that, so some things were in place," she said. She called, broke the news, and said, "Mom, I'm going to be all right."

To her surprise, Sarah got a reaction from her mom she hadn't expected: "Sarah, I know you'll be all right." Her job loss galvanized a relationship that had been shaky for years, and now she receives emotional support unlike anything she's ever known from her mom.

Unemployed children who are caring for or supporting their elderly parents face a tough situation. They probably don't have the luxury of waiting a week or more like Sarah did. They will need to break the news fairly soon after the announcement that they've lost their job, while reassuring their parents that everything will get back on track.

## WHAT TO TELL YOUR SPOUSE

"For richer for poorer . . ." Remember making that vow? You're about to learn about the "poorer" side of the equation. How you will work this out long-term remains to be seen. For now, you need to let your spouse know. When you explain what happened, be factual, clear, and dispassionate. Deal with these issues first:

☞ What actually happened when you got the word.
☞ How much more time you have before you must leave the company (if the termination wasn't that day).
☞ What you can reasonably expect in cash from your vacation, sick leave, severance, profit sharing, and any other monetary compensation from the company.
☞ How you will tell your parents, children, and any other relative or friend who needs to know.

You may not have a grasp yet on what these issues will mean for your family's lifestyle and plans. Don't worry about that now. You'll have plenty of time to assess those matters later.

The immediate emotional impact will depend on whether your spouse also works, whether you have children, if you are caring for elderly parents, as well as other factors such as marital difficulties or family indebtedness. Many families' budgets are stretched to the limit as it is, often because of large monthly mortgage payments. If both of you have been working to sustain the income level you need for basic survival, the overall economic impact will be similar no matter which of you becomes unemployed. Therefore, you share the same need for support in the event of losing your job.

But even though the economic impact is the same whether husband or wife loses a job, the loss usually hits the husband the hardest. Traditionally, he is expected to be the primary breadwinner for the family. The bread-eaters may feel as if he is letting them down, especially if unemployment drags on longer than a couple of months. If the wife is working, the shock is cushioned somewhat by a second breadwinner.

This isn't to say that job loss isn't devastating for the wife as well. Especially if she has been pursuing a career path, unemployment can be just as devastating for her as it is for him. Women often have to study and work harder than men for the same position and income. The emotional impact will be harder as well. The reality that she will have to try even harder all over again may cause her to suffer deep discouragement, which could work against her in the job hunt.

The economic consequences will be more immediate if only one of the married couple is a breadwinner. In most cases, that breadwinner is the husband. He will need his wife's support, but she may already have her hands full raising the children. Teamwork is essential in this case, especially if circumstances require the wife to look for a job as well.

## WHAT TO TELL YOUR BOYFRIEND, GIRLFRIEND, OR FIANCÉ

Unemployment could be the first or greatest test of either a young or mature romance. The announcement of a layoff or firing will rub the blush off a romance about as quickly as anything, especially if the jobless person has been in the working world for only a few years.

The method of telling the other follows the advice for married couples: Be factual and straightforward. You can gauge the depth of your relationship by the level of emotional support. Unemployment can shatter a person's well-being and inflame tension and anger. On the other hand, it can build deeper levels of caring. The relationship will also be tested by whether it can continue at a greatly reduced level of spending and entertainment.

Unemployment strains the relationship of engaged couples. The strain usually increases the further along the couple is in their wedding plans. The desire to marry sooner will probably be more intense when one is unemployed, in part because two can live more cheaply than one. But if delaying the wedding is possible, do so. Entering a marriage with a spouse out of work could put an unnecessary and inordinate stress on a delicate time. If delaying a wedding is neither possible nor desirable, the person out of work will need to be as diligent in finding a job as if he or she were still single. Unemployment is not an excuse for a prolonged honeymoon.

## WHAT TO TELL YOUR CHILDREN

When we experience job loss, we enter a grieving process. According to noted Denver-area child psychiatrist Dr. Foster W. Cline, how we convey our responses to our children while we're in this process is more important than the actual news itself. "It's not the *facts* of unemployment but the parents' *affects*," asserts Dr. Cline. "If parents are scared themselves, that's what comes through to the kids."

Dr. Cline recommends two basic practical ways parents can allay their children's fears.

1. Always tell the truth.
2. Let them know what is the worst possible thing that could happen—and then point out that in all likelihood, it *won't* happen. When you say, "Even if we lose the house, we'll always have a place to sleep," it will help your children realize, "Gee, if that's the worst, we can survive that."

You can gear the specifics of what you tell your children by taking into account that children's ages will have a bearing on their reactions. Here are some age-appropriate suggestions.

### Children Ages Two Years and Younger

Until children begin talking, you don't need to worry about how they will react to your actual loss, says Dr. Cline. However, little children can sense your emotional well-being when you touch and hold them. So as best as you can, be the happy parent you've always been.

### Children Ages Three to Five
Once children start talking, they can pick up what is going on at home, no matter how much parents hide or disguise it. They don't understand the details of what their parents do or what happened at work. But they take interest in such basic questions as, "Will we have enough to eat?"

Your best response is by reassuring them, "This is a tough time for mommy and daddy. We'll be spending a lot of time looking for a job. But don't worry, we love you and we'll always have enough to eat." That will settle most of the issues for this age group.

### Children Ages Six to Eighteen
Starting at about age five or six, children take a keen interest in what their parents do and where they work. You can't fool your children, so you should be truthful and clear about what happened. Explain unemployment in terms that your kids will understand, just as you discuss any other issue of growing up—from allowances to schoolwork to sex.

Acknowledge to your children that as an unemployed parent, you will experience more stress than usual. Explain that it's normal for parents to react to this kind of stress inappropriately sometimes—by losing their temper with their children, for example. This explanation can help "inoculate" children to your stress. Then when you lose your temper, your child can remember, "Oh, Mom told me she'd get like this. I'm not worried."

Realize that discussing your job loss with your children might make them feel uncomfortable. As an alternative, consider arranging for a third party to talk with them about it. Sources here could include a counselor or trusted adult identified through a church or community organization. Ask this adult to describe what has happened and give your child a chance to respond. With a trusted counselor readily available, the child can comfortably talk out his or her fears and concerns without feeling that he or she is burdening the family.

Dr. Cline points out that children older than five or six may face harassment from their peers about their parent's job loss. You can help your children endure their peers' barbs by telling them that teasing may happen, and asking them whether they can handle it. In most cases, the children will answer, "Yeah, I can handle it."

You can encourage your children to be ready with a response to their peers by putting an optimistic spin on your unemployment. Children can deflate teasing by saying, "My dad is looking real hard for a job, and he wants to find the best job he can." This will go much farther than saying, "My dad's out of work."

Under no circumstances should you force your children to lie about or cover for what is happening at home, warns Dr. Cline. This creates an ethical conflict for children and puts a burden of shame on them as well.

**Single Parents and Their Children**
Single parents already carry twice the burden of couples for caring for their families. Their nerves, energy, and budgets often hover near the breaking point. Unemployment may send single parents crashing into despair.

Single moms and single dads often develop support networks to help them through tough times. When single parents lose their jobs, they often do what Sarah did in the opening anecdote. Before breaking the news to her teenage son, she waited several hours to give herself a chance to calm down and get over the initial shock. Then she asked a friend to accompany her when she told her son that she had been fired. Her friend was able to absorb some of her son's anger and blunt the other emotional tensions that might have flared.

As best as possible, children need to be made aware that mom's or dad's unemployment will affect them personally. This shouldn't be communicated harshly, but it should get across the message that dad or mom will need all the help their children can give them.

"... FOR BETTER FOR WORSE . . ."
Say a prayer and give your loved ones a hug. Look them in the eye and let them know how much you care for them and love them. Be open to their love and support, especially when you want to withdraw. Such comfort will go far in the weeks and months ahead.

Now that you've taken the steps to secure an emotional foundation, you need to take a hard look at your finances. How well you survive your unemployment—and how well your family survives your unemployment—will greatly depend on this next step. Far too many engagements, marriages, and families founder on the rocks of poor or nonexistent financial planning. Historically, that's been true in the "for better" times. It's of utmost concern in the "for worse" times.

# CHAPTER FIVE

# Assessing Your Financial Situation

◆━◆

T he comfort of a regular paycheck can sometimes lull us into forgetting that we might be only a paycheck or two away from losing
the house, apartment, or car. As long as the money keeps coming in,
we're not always forced to pay close attention to where it's coming
from and where it's going. Spending habits become just that—habits.
We don't have to give them a whole lot of thought.

Once the paycheck stream dries up, we tend to panic. But this is
no time for panic. What we most need at this point is to think very
clearly and soberly about how to handle ourselves and our money. We
need to conduct a careful and honest—brutally honest—assessment of
our financial situation.

The party's over (if there ever was one in the first place). Getting
a grip on finances starts *now*. If you're not controlling your money,
your money's controlling you. The sooner you deal with this reality,
the better off you'll be in shoring up your self-esteem, maintaining your
relationships, and developing confidence and clear thinking as you look
for a new job or career.

IGNORANCE IS NOT BLISS
I worked as a reporter in southeast Texas at the height of the recession
following the oil bust of the early and mid-1980s. Until then, money
had been flowing as fast and slick as the black gold from the oil patch.
But unlike the globs of crude occasionally washed ashore on the Texas
beaches, money didn't stick to wage-earners.

I spoke with financial advisors to families whose breadwinners had lost their jobs in the petrochemical and support industries. Many families had combined annual incomes ranging from $50,000 to $70,000 and more. But they had little to show for it: few savings, no investments, no retirement funds. So the advisors suggested that these families raise cash by selling their boats, their cabins on the lake, their second cars. The response they frequently got back was, "Why?"

Money greatly affects our daily lives. But we don't often talk about how it affects us. Or how we use it. Maybe we're hoping that if we ignore those issues long enough, they'll go away—or at least not embarrass us.

But this kind of ignorance is not bliss. Especially if you're unemployed or at risk for losing your job, this ignorance could devastate you. It's not just a damaged credit rating or even the loss of a home waiting in the wings of possibilities, but a ruinous blow to your personal life and your plans for the future. Even if you think a new job is around the corner, it is essential that you revamp your budget, corral all sources of income, cut your expenses, and think clearly about all financial decisions.

I now realize I made some serious errors during my first six months of unemployment, and the several months preceding it when I had the opportunity to prepare. Some simple changes in my lifestyle could have saved me several thousand dollars and a lot of anxiety. For example, I didn't start cutting back immediately when I received the notice of my dismissal. I rented business equipment when I could have bought better equipment for the same money. And I turned down the opportunity to move into a cheaper apartment in the same building because I didn't think I would be out of work for very long.

This chapter suggests guidelines for analyzing your cash flow, insurance, investments, and taxes. These suggestions have been culled from financial planners, the experiences of others, and common sense. Additionally, financial counseling is available through the nationwide network of Consumer Credit Counseling Services, which offers seminars geared for those who have just lost their jobs. Numerous books are available at your local library that examine these issues in greater depth. The steps outlined here and in following chapters will help you start doing more with less, avoid making foolish mistakes, resist despair, and above all think clearly.

## CASH MANAGEMENT

One of the most important principles of cash management is, *Every dollar you have is precious*. You may remember your parents referring to "knowing the value of a dollar"—which at the time you may have sarcastically dismissed as "quaint." Now you are about to learn the value of a dollar, and just how un-quaint that is. The steps are simple. The discipline of living by them isn't. But this effort will help you survive unemployment and change your lifestyle for a long time to come.

### Making a Budget

If you've been keeping a budget, you're off to a head start. If you've never done it, now is a great time to learn. It's also essential for surviving unemployment.

You don't need a fancy system to follow the steps in getting started. Figure 5-1 provides a sample monthly budget sheet. You can also obtain record-keeping systems from office supply stores, create your own form with a ledger pad, or use a computer software program for home budgeting.

**FIGURE 5-1  SAMPLE BUDGET**

|  | TOTAL FAMILY | SELF | SPOUSE |
|---|---|---|---|
| **Income** | | | |
| Salary/wages | $_____ | $_____ | $_____ |
| Social Security | $_____ | $_____ | $_____ |
| Pension | $_____ | $_____ | $_____ |
| Interest | $_____ | $_____ | $_____ |
| Dividends | $_____ | $_____ | $_____ |
| Rents | $_____ | $_____ | $_____ |
| Sale of investments | $_____ | $_____ | $_____ |
| Alimony | $_____ | $_____ | $_____ |
| Child support | $_____ | $_____ | $_____ |
| Other _____ | $_____ | $_____ | $_____ |
| Other _____ | $_____ | $_____ | $_____ |
| Other _____ | $_____ | $_____ | $_____ |
| TOTAL INCOME | $_____ | $_____ | $_____ |

*(figure 5-1 continued on next page)*

FIGURE 5-1 SAMPLE BUDGET *(CONTINUED)*

| | TOTAL FAMILY | SELF | SPOUSE |
|---|---|---|---|
| **Expenses** | | | |
| Savings | $_____ | $_____ | $_____ |
| Investments | $_____ | $_____ | $_____ |
| Retirement savings | $_____ | $_____ | $_____ |
| Income taxes | $_____ | $_____ | $_____ |
| Property taxes | $_____ | $_____ | $_____ |
| Insurance (life) | $_____ | $_____ | $_____ |
| Insurance (health) | $_____ | $_____ | $_____ |
| Insurance (auto) | $_____ | $_____ | $_____ |
| Insurance (other) | $_____ | $_____ | $_____ |
| Medical | $_____ | $_____ | $_____ |
| Dental | $_____ | $_____ | $_____ |
| Food (groceries) | $_____ | $_____ | $_____ |
| Food (meals out) | $_____ | $_____ | $_____ |
| Utilities | $_____ | $_____ | $_____ |
| Telephone | $_____ | $_____ | $_____ |
| Loan _____ | $_____ | $_____ | $_____ |
| Loan _____ | $_____ | $_____ | $_____ |
| Loan _____ | $_____ | $_____ | $_____ |
| Credit card payments | $_____ | $_____ | $_____ |
| Day/child care | $_____ | $_____ | $_____ |
| Education | $_____ | $_____ | $_____ |
| Subscriptions | $_____ | $_____ | $_____ |
| Clothing | $_____ | $_____ | $_____ |
| Cleaning | $_____ | $_____ | $_____ |
| Recreation | $_____ | $_____ | $_____ |
| Gifts | $_____ | $_____ | $_____ |
| Donations | $_____ | $_____ | $_____ |
| Other _____ | $_____ | $_____ | $_____ |
| Other _____ | $_____ | $_____ | $_____ |
| Other _____ | $_____ | $_____ | $_____ |
| | | | |
| TOTAL EXPENSES | $_____ | $_____ | $_____ |

**Total income** ($_____) – **Total expenses** ($_____) = $_____

The budget sheet included here will help you begin accounting for your monthly income and expenses. If you are new at this, make several copies of this sheet and get your checkbook, bills, statements, and receipts for the past three months. For each month, list what you have spent in each of these categories. Average the totals for each category. Add the totals for income and expenses. Now, take a deep breath and subtract your total expenses from your total income.

This sum shows where you have been in your cash management. Like other journeys in life, you'll have a hard time knowing where you're going if you don't know where you've been.

Now, get several more copies of this or a similar budgeting sheet. Tally the income you think you will have for the next several months. Enter that in the "other" categories. This will be tentative until you know what and how much severance, vacation pay, and other money you will receive from your employer (if any); whether you will qualify for unemployment insurance benefits; and if you think you may become self-employed or find part-time or temporary work. Remember that this estimate is a forecast. If you plan expenses against income that you really aren't sure you will have, you're only fooling yourself.

### Determining What You Can Cut

Now you're ready for the hard decisions and the cost-cutting. Be creative in determining what you can cut. Surviving unemployment will mean breaking old patterns of thinking about income and expenses. Remember the old Yankee maxim: "Use it up, wear it out. Make it do or do without."

If your children are old enough, involve them in determining what gets cut, suggests child psychiatrist Dr. Foster Cline. "The more children are involved in a decision, the better. Everybody in the family will have to give up some stuff," he advises. Unemployment will hurt everyone, just as new employment will benefit everyone.

Brainstorm with your family about what else you can do. Note how much you can save for each category. For example, if you have been paying $25 a month for cable television, you can pay $0 in your new budget. Those cuts will add up. (For further details on how to make do with less, see chapter 10.) Other suggestions for trimming your budget:

*Housing.* If you own your residence, stay in touch with your lender. Explain your situation *before* you ever miss a payment. Talk to your lender about the possibility of refinancing your mortgage.

If you rent, stay in touch with your landlord. Consider changing rental units, but weigh relocation costs carefully. Moving may mean breaking a lease, transferring utilities, incurring moving costs (unless you have a friend with a pickup truck), and transferring children to another school. But if you can save at least $100 to $200 in rent, the move will pay for itself in several months.

*Other lenders.* As with your mortgage lender or landlord, it's important to contact your other lenders, such as the one who holds your car loan.

Some loan holders, especially student loan lenders, may allow you to apply for an unemployment deferment. The lender may grant the student loan deferments for as many as twenty-four months, but you must reapply for the deferment at regular intervals. If you qualify for a deferment, you must be able to show that you've made a conscientious effort to find full-time work. Contact your lender for more details.

*Utilities.* Practice energy conservation. Turn down the heat. Turn down (or off) the air conditioner. Keep appliance use to a minimum. Don't water the lawn. Eliminate cable TV. Make long-distance phone calls for job hunting and emergencies only!

*Food.* Eliminate snack foods, prepared foods, and alcoholic beverages. Cut back or eliminate meat consumption. Clip and use coupons. Don't eat out.

*Transportation.* If your automobile is financed, let your lender know of your situation. Ride your bike or use public transportation if available. Shop for gas prices. Keep fluid levels full to eliminate breakdowns. Delay all repairs that don't affect the safety or legality of the car.

*Clothes.* Don't buy any new clothes. Buy necessary items, such as children's clothes, at garage sales or thrift shops. Exchange clothes with other families. Limit wearing of clothes that require dry cleaning, such as the suit you wear for job interviews.

*Entertainment.* Let magazine and newspaper subscriptions lapse. Cut out concerts, first-run movies, ball games. Drop social club memberships unless you can honestly say to yourself that you will use the clubs for networking. Cancel the family vacation. Explore free or low-cost activities in your community.

*Charitable contributions.* Balanced against your primary duty to provide for yourself and your family, follow your personal conviction in deciding what level of charitable giving to maintain. You might even need to rely on the charity of others to see you through this rough time. Remember that after you find work again, you will have plenty of opportunities to return the favors. Consider volunteering as a substitute for giving to charity.

*Day care*. Cancel day care if you will be doing most of your job hunting by phone from your home. Make arrangements with relatives or friends who may be able to take care of your children when you go out for job hunting and interviews.

## Raising Cash

If you can't live on your current income even after cutting back expenses and setting up a stringent new budget, then you need to look at other income possibilities, such as temporary or part-time work. This type of work may not be what you want, and it may not pay well, but right now the important thing is to meet your expenses. Do not list this income on your budget until you actually have acquired these resources.

Here are some suggestions for raising cash or other needed resources.

1. *Part-time work*. Restaurants and retail stores may be good prospects for part-time employment. Check newspaper classified ads.

2. *Temporary work*. Temporary help agencies that do not charge a fee can help you find a position utilizing your skills. Some also provide training in other skills. You may find opportunities for seasonal work during the holidays. If you have a college degree, consider checking with local school districts about substitute teaching (certification may not be a requirement).

3. *Self-employment*. Consider skills you may be able to market: child care, lawn care, catering, writing, bookkeeping, house repair, or consulting. (See also chapter 14 for more help on items 1-3.)

4. *Unemployment insurance benefits*. Refigure your budget after the state determines your qualification for unemployment insurance benefits. (See also chapter 6.)

5. *Donations from charitable organizations*. Cash, groceries, and clothing may be available from local agencies or religious organizations. (See also chapter 11.)

6. *Investments*. See the following section on liquid and illiquid investments.

7. *Retirement*. If you are able to roll over a 401-K or other company retirement plan into an Individual Retirement Account (IRA), do so. If you can cash out the retirement plan without paying any penalties, consider

that, too. But remember that you may owe income tax on this cash.

8. *Savings*. Comb your records for any savings you may have forgotten. Check with your insurance agent about cash value and liquidity of your insurance policies.

9. *Taking out a loan*. Borrowing money to survive unemployment should be a last resort whether from a financial institution or family members. Even if you—despite your jobless status—are able to arrange a loan with a financial institution, you face the discouragement of repaying it after you find work again. Although by now you've informed your family about your unemployment, you should wait to borrow from them until you've explored all other options. If you do borrow, make explicit arrangements to repay them.

10. *Other*. Hold a garage sale to eliminate unused household items. (This is especially useful in preparing for a possible relocation.) Sell large items, such as appliances or a second car. Rent out a spare room or garage. (Check with the Internal Revenue Service before proceeding, because rental income is reported on Schedule E.)

CREDIT MANAGEMENT

Right now, credit can be your friend or foe. It is always important to use credit wisely, especially when you're unemployed. Suggestions:

1. *Put away or destroy all credit cards,* except a major bank card such as VISA or MasterCard. If using a credit card for some expenses—such as gasoline—helps with budgeting, by all means use it—as long as you don't abuse the opportunity and you can pay it off in full every month.

2. *If your unemployment is at least several months away, pay off or reduce as many current balances as possible.* For balances you cannot pay off, pay only the monthly minimum. Always pay something! Contact those creditors you might have trouble paying (see appendix A on page 215 for a sample letter). Never ignore any creditor.

3. *Use the bank card for emergencies only,* such as a new water heater, furnace repair, car repair, and emergency transportation. Use your credit card for cash withdrawals only if you already have made a habit of entering the withdrawals in your checkbook or other record-keeping files.

4. *If you're still employed but your job looks risky, consider purchasing credit card insurance.* With some credit card companies, the insurance will cover the monthly minimum payment if you lose your

job, and you may still be able to use the card. Again, use credit cards only in emergencies.

5. *Some creditors will allow a month's grace period for missing a payment.* However, don't resort to this until you absolutely have no other recourse. In such extreme situations, it may buy you another thirty to sixty days. But once you use it, it's gone.

6. *If your bills become overwhelming, seek help through low-cost or no-cost advice such as Consumer Credit Counseling Service or other similar organizations.*

Consumer debt may be one of the most frightening monsters you face as unemployment wears on. Credit can be a wonderful luxury, but its abuse has driven thousands of people to despair and bankruptcy. The National Foundation for Consumer Credit was established more than forty years ago to help people cope with their debts, learn to use credit wisely, and develop personal responsibility for managing their finances.

The foundation sponsors more than seven hundred Consumer Credit Counseling Services in the U.S. and Canada, which offer confidential and professional financial counseling. These programs have helped thousands of people avoid bankruptcy, wage garnishment, and foreclosure by helping them to think clearly and gain control over their finances. These non-profit services focus on helping people cope with credit crises, but they also offer seminars for those who have just lost their jobs, money management workshops, debt counseling, housing counseling, and other programs.

Most programs charge a minimal fee, usually on a sliding scale depending on ability to pay. (About a third of CCCS programs are free.) Most cities and regions have their own Consumer Credit Counseling Service. Contacting a Consumer Credit Counseling Service now could save you thousands of dollars, as well as your credit rating and even your home.

INSURANCE

During tough financial times it is very tempting to cut out insurance coverage. *Don't do it.* Not only could inadequate insurance coverage be very costly, in some instances (especially with automobiles) it even may be illegal. If you drop your insurance, you are gambling with your savings and long-term financial health. If you suffer a catastrophe, the gambling losses could be severe.

## Health Insurance

Health insurance is critical. You are gambling with your family's health and your life savings if you're unemployed and don't carry medical insurance.

Legally, most employees who are voluntarily or involuntarily terminated (for reasons other than gross misconduct) are entitled to continue health coverage at group rates for eighteen months and possibly longer. This right was guaranteed by the Consolidated Omnibus Budget Reconciliation Act of 1986 (COBRA), which covers group health plans maintained by employers of more than twenty employees. Spouses and dependent children also benefit from the requirements of COBRA. Coverage may include doctor care, inpatient and outpatient hospital care, major medical expenses, prescription drugs, and possible dental and vision care. The former employee must pay the premiums (sometimes with a small surcharge). However, you may want to shop around for a more affordable plan, or a plan with a higher deductible.

## Life Insurance

Unemployed people often target life insurance coverage for elimination. Before you ignore the next premium notice, consider the importance of life insurance. If you have dependents, it is essential to continue the coverage. Check with your insurance agent to learn if your policy has any cash accumulation. If there is enough cash in the account, you may be able to apply it to the premium.

If you carry term policy with no cash build-up, check with your agent about paying in monthly or quarterly installments instead of semi-annually or annually, to stretch out the payments. The total premium may not be cheaper, but it will help with monthly budgeting.

If you have numerous life insurance policies, consider consolidating all the policies into one. One policy for a hundred thousand dollars' benefit will be cheaper than ten polices of ten thousand dollars each. Remember, if you drop all of your coverage, future medical conditions may make future life insurance very expensive or unavailable.

## Property and Casualty Insurance

You should keep your property and casualty insurance, too. Property insurance protects your assets against major loss or damage. It also protects you if somebody is hurt on your property, or by your automobile.

## Homeowner's and Renter's Insurance

For most people, a house is probably their single largest asset. Replacing your house and/or its contents could be very costly. If your house is financed, your lender requires that the investment be covered. If you rent, continue your renter's insurance to protect your possessions and to insulate you from lawsuits.

Regardless of whether you own or rent, if you haven't recently analyzed your policy or shopped for coverage, you have an excellent opportunity now to shop for cheaper coverage.

## Automobile Insurance

Your automobile is a major tool for modern living, and it will be necessary for job hunting. You need coverage to protect your car from damage and liability coverage to protect you from lawsuits. Also, in most states, it is illegal to drive without liability insurance. If your car is financed, the lender requires the car to be covered by comprehensive and collision insurance.

To lower your automobile insurance costs, consider raising your comprehensive and collision deductibles to $500. If your car is more than five years old (and paid for), you might want to consider dropping the comprehensive or collision coverage or both. Do not drop your liability coverage. Again, now may be an excellent time to shop for cheaper coverage.

## INVESTMENTS AND RETIREMENT PLANS

### Liquid Investments

Liquid investments are those investments that can readily be converted to cash. They include certificates of deposit, stocks, bonds, savings bonds, mutual funds, and life insurance cash values.

If you need to raise cash during your unemployment, you need to evaluate which investment to liquidate. Weigh the costs if you liquidate early. Some investments, such as certificates of deposit or insurance products, are subject to penalty for early withdrawal. When liquidating stocks, bonds, or mutual funds, market conditions are important. A poor market could force you to sell out when prices are low, thus taking a loss on your investments. However, if you need the cash to keep your health insurance or to protect a longer-term investment such as your house by paying the monthly mortgage bill, you may not have an option other than to liquidate.

## Illiquid Investments

Illiquid investments are assets for which there is not a readily available market, such as real estate, business interests, or collectibles. These investments can take a long time to liquidate, and an acceptable price may be difficult to obtain.

Before liquidating any investment, you must decide if you can do without the investment or if you should look at other alternatives of raising cash, such as temporary or part-time work.

## Retirement Plans

Retirement plans such as Individual Retirement Accounts (IRAs) and distributions from company retirement plans (deferred compensation, also known as 401-Ks) should be considered long-term, illiquid investments. Consider your future financial security against the need for short-term cash. If you cash out of the plan early, you could interfere with your long-term retirement goals, pay penalties for early withdrawal, and owe federal income tax. Once you take that money out, you cannot replace it.

Remember that your unemployment is a temporary problem. It's not worth sacrificing long-term security for what probably will be a short-term hardship. By disciplining yourself to save in ways other than tapping into your retirement funds, you also have the emotional satisfaction of building resources to live on in the future.

## TAXES

Preparing to file your taxes starts now. You can save yourself headaches, if not money, by planning ahead for the next April 15. Uncle Sam hasn't lost interest in you, even if you've lost your job. Unemployment is not an excuse for not filing. And failure to file will cost you in penalties, possible legal recrimination, and wasted time down the road.

## Record-keeping

You already know that careful record-keeping is the best aspirin for tax-time headaches. Many of the issues surrounding unemployment and searching for new employment require special income tax reporting, such as job hunting costs, selling your house, and relocation expenses.

Keep written records, including receipts, to substantiate all expenses and activities for job hunting. A lost receipt means a lost deduction. Canceled checks are usually as good as receipts, although not always. The Internal Revenue Service has publications available to help you with record-keeping and tax matters. They are available from local IRS offices or by calling the 800 telephone numbers for the IRS listed in your phone book.

## Income Taxes

Current tax regulations consider unemployment insurance benefits to be ordinary taxable income. If you do part-time or temporary work, make sure that enough federal and state income taxes are withheld not only to cover that income, but your unemployment insurance benefits as well.

If you decide to go into business for yourself—even when you are looking for employment with another company—you must report income and expenses on Schedule C when you file federal income tax.

If you liquidate investments or retirement plans, these require special IRS income tax reporting, too.

## Property Taxes

Most people who have a mortgage have property tax figured into their monthly payment. Most mortgage lenders will set up the property taxes and property insurance in an escrow account that's part of your mortgage payment. Consequently, you have a level monthly payment, which in turn helps you with monthly budgeting.

If property taxes aren't factored into your payment, you must budget money for property taxes due at the end of the year. Don't miss this payment. If you miss the payment, the county will notify your lender, who in turn notifies you. You don't want to risk this.

## SHOULD YOU FILE FOR BANKRUPTCY?

Filings for personal bankruptcy have climbed relentlessly in recent years. The stigma of bankruptcy has faded, but the consequences haven't. Sure, filing in federal bankruptcy courts can protect you from harassment from creditors and foreclosure on your house (in many instances). But your credit rating probably will be damaged severely for as long as a decade. In our economy, a good credit rating is paramount for everything from renting a car to buying a house.

Bankruptcy is major. It's bad news for you and your family. Filing for bankruptcy is a long-term answer for what may be a short-term problem of unemployment. You don't know what the next ten years will hold.

An example of the consequences of bankruptcy could be your teen's inability to get a student loan because your previous filing for bankruptcy disqualifies you to co-sign the loan. Other problems include difficulty in obtaining favorable rates when you try to buy a car, apply for a credit card, rent an apartment, and especially buy a house.

Seek every possible solution before you think of calling a bankruptcy lawyer. Get your budget in line, cut all possible expenses, contact your creditors, seek help from a credit counseling service. Bankruptcy simply isn't worth the pain, even the pain of unemployment.

## GETTING ON YOUR FEET

Deal with your finances with honesty and integrity. Be honest with yourself, your family, and your creditors. At best, dishonesty will perpetuate an illusion of prosperity—or at least financial status quo—which is psychologically stressful. At worst, it will land you in court.

Now that you're getting a grip on managing your finances and planning for the months ahead, you have one final step to take in the initial process of surviving unemployment: filing for unemployment insurance benefits. An understanding of what unemployment insurance is, how to file for it, and what to expect from it will give you a leg up on those dreary scenes on the evening news that we all hope won't ever include us. But many of us who have lost our jobs go through this rite of passage. Let's get an insider's view of how to help take the sting out of it.

# CHAPTER SIX

# Filing for Unemployment Insurance Benefits

◆

Y ou really know you're out of work when you stand in an unemployment line for the first time. There's no better cure for that smugness you may have felt while watching long lines in unemployment offices on TV than finding yourself part of that same picture.

By now you should realize that unemployment is not shameful. Neither is filing for unemployment insurance benefits. However, standing in line and listening to lectures on how to fill out the forms can feel pretty dehumanizing. But if you stay calm and know what to do, you can save yourself time and headaches.

Once you step into the unemployment office, you are dealing with a bureaucracy of the state government. However, that doesn't mean it's insensitive. "We run this program as a business," said Don Peitersen, director of the Colorado Department of Labor & Employment. "People aren't claimants, they're customers. They've got to be treated like anybody in any business. Each and every one of us is a customer of government services."

Peitersen himself has drawn unemployment insurance benefits, as have other people behind the desk or on the phone at unemployment offices. In other words, you're not alone with your questions or frustrations. When you file, treat your representative as you want to be treated. That will go far to alleviate the anxiety you feel, and it will make the whole process run much more smoothly.

States are trying to make the process run more smoothly, too, Peitersen remarked. "This program has been good at putting up barriers to prevent people from asking questions," he admitted. In most states, the only way to get answers is to visit the Job Service centers, which often don't take phone calls. That will be changing drastically in the next few years.

Colorado, for example, has set up an 800 number so people can file for unemployment insurance over the phone. Operators receive the claim, enter the information into a computer, print out the form, and mail it to the caller. The 800 number also allows questions to be handled over the phone, relieving individuals of the necessity of making a trip to the unemployment office just to get information. This phone system is the wave of the future, Peitersen predicted, pointing out that other states are currently considering similar programs. "What this system does is allow people to conduct unemployment business on *their* time, not the state's time," he explained.

Whether or not your state has a phone system, it does incorporate similar policies and procedures. Each state has its own policies and publishes its own unemployment insurance handbook—get hold of one and *read it thoroughly!* In the meantime, before you deal with the specifics of your state's program, you can become familiar with the kinds of steps you need to follow to minimize the hassles. (Much of the advice in this chapter was suggested by Don Peitersen.)

## THE UNEMPLOYMENT INSURANCE SYSTEM
### What Is Unemployment Insurance?
Unemployment insurance is a partial temporary wage replacement for individuals who are unemployed through no fault of their own. This includes workers in the public and private sectors and military personnel. (Some types of firms, however, do not contribute to the unemployment insurance system. If you have any questions about your eligibility, contact your unemployment office.) To qualify for the benefits, you must meet two eligibility requirements:

1. You must meet a stipulated minimum level of monetary earnings at your former employment in order to qualify.
2. You must have lost your job and be actively seeking new employment.

### How Is the System Set Up, and Who Pays for It?
Your unemployment insurance is funded by two taxes paid by your employer. The first, mandated by the Federal Unemployment Tax

Act (FUTA), pays for the administration of the program. Levied by the Internal Revenue Service, it is 6.2 percent on the first $7,000 of your wages, less 5.4 percent on those wages as long as the state's program meets federal certification. Usually, then, the tax amounts to .8 percent on your first $7,000, or $56 per employee. That money goes to Washington, D.C., and from there it's distributed to the states. Part of the money goes into an account for extended benefits, and another account covers loans to states if their unemployment insurance funds go broke. The third part is for the administrative costs of unemployment insurance and the employment service (often called Job Service).

The second tax on employers is levied by the individual states for their unemployment insurance trust funds. That money pays for your benefits. The tax rate is variable from state to state, as well as from employer to employer. Employers who manage their work forces well, and consequently lay off or fire fewer employees, will pay less into the program because fewer employees file for benefits. Employers who don't manage their employees effectively will pay more.

The U.S. Congress gives the states latitude on how to run their own programs. Some states are tougher than others about what they require from employers and employees.

### What Percentage of Unemployed People Receive Unemployment Insurance Benefits?

For a variety of reasons, only about half the people who lose their jobs file for unemployment insurance benefits, Peitersen said. Some don't want the hassle. Some don't want to be seen at the unemployment office. "A lot of professional people say, 'I'm not going to deal with that riffraff,'" he explained. Others, who are convinced they'll find a job soon, assume they won't need the benefits.

Not all who apply for benefits qualify for them, either. Some people who are unemployed don't receive the insurance benefits because they don't apply to begin with. But about 80 percent of those who do apply receive benefits, he said.

STEPS TO TAKE WHEN YOU FILE

### Where Do I Go, or What Number Do I Call?

To contact the appropriate office, look in the phone book under Job Service, your state's department of labor and employment, or the state economic development office. Be sure to take the steps outlined below before you call or visit the unemployment office.

## When Should I Go to the Unemployment Office or Call the State Agency?

Filing for unemployment insurance is one of the rare times in the process of surviving unemployment when doing something too soon can cause you trouble. That's because the unemployment insurance process depends on your not having a job. Therefore, call or visit the office as soon as you leave your employer, *not before then.* The state agency cannot begin the process of determining whether you are eligible for benefits until your work ends.

In *every* case of filing for unemployment insurance benefits, the state agency contacts the employer for whom you claim to have worked. When you file before you leave your company, your employer will still have you on its rolls, so you obviously don't qualify for benefits, and the claim will be disallowed. That disallowance may come back to haunt you when you file again, after you have parted company with your employer.

## How Should I Prepare for Filing and Filling Out the Forms?

Careful and detailed preparation for filing is critical if you are to get through the process with the least trouble.

Most of the forms are fairly self-explanatory. They're similar to an application for a credit card. The questions are fairly simple, but like many of the simple things in life, we tend to forget them because they're so obvious. Every state will require this information. Be prepared with the following when you visit or call the unemployment office:

☞ Your Social Security card or some identification with your Social Security number on it. Your Social Security number will be entered into the computer system, and it will be the number by which you are identified when you call or visit the office.

☞ Know the exact name and street address of the employer you worked for. Jotting down "the ad agency on Third Street" won't get you very far.

☞ Know the exact names and street addresses of all other employers you've had for at least the past eighteen months.

☞ Specify the exact dates on which you started and ended

working for each of these past employers.
☞ Recount your salary history.

With this information in hand, you then need to be prepared to answer these questions:

☞ Are you a U.S. citizen? If not, can you present the appropriate information to prove your alien status?
☞ Are you a veteran?
☞ Are you drawing Social Security benefits?
☞ Are you drawing workers' compensation?
☞ Have you filed a claim for unemployment insurance benefits in any other state, and are you collecting benefits?

You also need to be prepared to answer what other income you received from your former employer: severance; vacation, maternity, and holiday pay; wages-in-lieu of notice; lump sum payments; Social Security benefits; pension or retirement programs you cashed out when you left; workers' compensation; back pay; earnings; and commissions.

Finally, you need to be prepared to answer what happened between you and your former employer. Practice writing out a description of what occurred, several times, before you visit the unemployment office or call the state agency to file your claim. Be rational and concise, and keep the emotional outbursts to yourself. The effort will save you time.

**Tips on Filling Out the Forms**
I hate filling out forms. I tend to be a perfectionist and seize up when faced with questions and blank spaces. Unemployment insurance forms were no different for me. However, like so many bureaucratic challenges in life, such forms can be conquered by staying calm and having patience.

Most states present lectures and/or audiovisual programs to guide you through the step-by-step procedure of filing. Listen, take notes, and don't hesitate to ask if you have any questions. It's okay to ask others if they've had experience in filling out the forms.

Start by reading over the claim form to get a feel for the questions. Concisely and truthfully answer each one.

You will be asked about your name and current address, the name of your spouse, the names of your dependent children, and whether you are required to pay alimony or child support.

The stickiest part of filing the claim occurs when you are asked why you left your former job. Don Peitersen said you'll have the easiest time answering this question if you've been laid off or furloughed.

Difficulties arise with people who quit or are fired, he said. If you quit, you need to know the exact reasons. It's not necessarily true that you don't qualify for benefits if you quit your job. There may have been circumstances that made it impossible for you to continue working there. Since you're the one who quit, only you know the reason. If you quit, you need to be consistent in your answers.

If you were fired, you need to know exactly why, and clearly state the reason. Don't worry about what you think your ex-employer will say about what happened when the state representative contacts them. The important thing for you is to answer the questions honestly.

Because of the large volume of claims the state receives, you will not be required to supply evidence when you file. The state will take your statement, your ex-employer's statement, and then compare them. In the minority of cases in which there is a conflict, the state will ask more questions. If the state denies your claim, then the appeals process starts, and you will need to bring in witnesses and evidence.

### Proper Behavior at the Unemployment Office

As you already know, job loss is a very emotional experience. But don't walk into the unemployment office thinking that the people behind the desks can help you with your family or financial woes. That's not their job. They're not qualified to give counseling. Check your emotions at the door so you'll be able to answer the questions factually with as little hassle as possible.

The biggest behavioral obstacle, said Don Peitersen, is when people come into the office with the perception, "I'm entitled to these benefits," and then get antagonistic with the personnel behind the desks. Be brief but clear about what happened to you.

Remember that the unemployment office is not a bank. Few states distribute the benefits from the unemployment office, so don't think that filing is a matter of telling someone, "I'm out of work," and then going to the next window to get your check. Some unemployed persons mistakenly assume that unemployment officers simply reach into a cash box and hand out the benefits.

Finally, minimize your distractions and behave with dignity:

☞ Leave your children with a friend. If that's not possible, make sure they bring a quiet toy to play with or something to read while you wait in line.

☞ Don't bring friends along, unless they were laid off at the same time you were.

☞ Consider bringing along something to read, because the lines can be long.

☞ Don't bother showing up if you're intoxicated or feeling belligerent.

**Keep Your Own Records**
As much as possible, make copies of everything you submit to the unemployment office, especially the biweekly claim cards. Make sure you're able to verify everything you write, whether on the initial application, subsequent documents, earnings log in the unemployment handbook, and especially the claim forms.

It's your responsibility to keep track of the names of former employers and other information. The more information you can provide if questions arise, the better off you are. If names and addresses can't be substantiated, you will lose your benefits and you will have to pay back what benefits you received.

OTHER QUESTIONS
**What Are the Rules Regarding Taxation on Unemployment Insurance?**
*All* unemployment benefits are subject to federal and (where applicable) state income taxes. It used to be the case that these benefits were either not taxed or taxed only in part: no longer. The state will send you a Form 1099-G stating the compensation you received. The state also sends a copy to the Internal Revenue Service, so don't think the IRS will forget about it.

If you do find employment after you've been receiving unemployment benefits, ask your new employer to withhold more taxes on your W-4 form. That way, you won't owe as much next April 15.

**What Is Job Service? How Do I Register for It?**
The employment service known as Job Service (or a similar name) is the labor market exchange of the unemployment compensation program. This is the heartbeat of the program, because the whole point is

to get people back to work; unemployment insurance is the safety net to provide assistance in the meantime. After you file a claim for benefits, you will probably receive a notice to register with Job Service.

The chief requirement of receiving benefits is that you maintain an active job search, including through Job Service. When you register with Job Service, usually at the same location as the unemployment office, you place your name in a computer bank that tries to match you and your skills with whatever employment may be available. You may also be eligible for workshops to help you with your search, filling out job applications, writing résumés, and learning interviewing techniques.

In addition to Job Service, you are required to seek work actively in the best ways you know how, through networking, classified ads, sending out résumés, and other means. You will arrange with the unemployment office to make a specific number of job contacts a week, usually at least one to three, but maybe more. Keep accurate records of your contacts. You need to inform the agency if you've refused a job. You are allowed to refuse work if it isn't comparable to the job you had. But there are penalties for refusing to accept suitable work when it is offered.

### What Is "Job Attached" Status?

Some companies lay off workers temporarily, asking them to return after a specified period of time, often within eight weeks. Construction workers face this issue frequently. If you fall into such a category, you may apply for "job attached" status on your claim. This means your employer is certifying that the company will have a job for you in a certain amount of time. You might also be job attached if you find work through a union hiring hall. This status relieves the claimant of the responsibility to look for work.

### WHAT TO EXPECT AFTER FILING

### What Happens Next?

After you file, the state agency reviews your claim and checks with your former employer. Usually you will qualify for benefits if you lost your job through no fault of your own, are able to prove that you quit because of mitigating circumstances, or were fired without cause. You will receive by mail a statement announcing that you qualified for benefits and specifying how much you will receive.

The weekly benefit amount is usually determined by a "base period"—an average of how much you earned in the first four of the last five quarterly periods before you filed. Each state has its own minimum and maximum weekly benefits, based on the average weekly wage in the state. The more you earned in the base period before you lost your job, the greater the weekly benefit amount you will receive.

The total value of benefits you are allowed will probably be twenty-six times the weekly benefit amount. If, for example, your weekly benefit amount is $190, the total value of your benefits will be $4,940. You can claim those benefits over a fifty-two-week period called a "benefit year." It is to your advantage to spread out the twenty-six weeks of benefits for the fifty-two-week year.

You can do that by earning money. For example, in Colorado you can earn as much as 25 percent of your weekly benefit amount before it affects your benefits. If you have a part-time job, you can earn as much as $47.50 a week (25 percent of the $190 example) over your weekly benefit amount of $190 (for a total of $237.50) without losing any unemployment insurance benefits that week. However, any income *over* that amount will reduce your weekly benefits on a dollar-for-dollar basis.

To continue the example, if you earn $100 a week, you will collect $137.50 in unemployment insurance benefits ($190 minus $52.50, the amount exceeding 25 percent of your benefit). This state's division of unemployment insurance will retain the $52.50 in benefits you didn't collect that week for your future use. Because the total value of your benefits remains constant, you can therefore stretch out the number of weeks you receive benefits. (Other states may have different ways of calculating earnings and benefits.)

It is illegal to earn income and not report it. If you are caught, at the least you will have to pay back what you received. At the worst, you could be prosecuted.

If you are the one responsible for being out of work, you will probably be disqualified from receiving benefits. But you will be allowed to appeal that decision.

### How Long Does It Take for Unemployment Insurance to Begin?

Normally, unemployment insurance takes three to four weeks to go into effect. The first of those weeks is a waiting week, which doesn't qualify for any benefits.

Don Peitersen explained that although people are upset that the process takes this long, the state has the obligation to check with the ex-employer. It's easier for a state to process claims based on layoffs, because often many people lose their jobs at once, and the ex-employer doesn't contest the ex-employees' claims. But when the claim load rises, such as after a massive layoff or during a recession, delays occur.

### What Are the Problems and/or Penalties for Filing False Claims?

Although the amounts vary, each state imposes penalties on both the employer and the employee if either files a false claim. The system *does* police itself, so don't file a false claim. You will be caught and required to give back what you were overpaid. And you might very well be prosecuted, fined, and jailed. In other words, if you do the crime, you'll do the time.

If an ex-employer files a false claim, the state can award a claimant a surplus beyond what the employee is entitled to, and the state can take legal action against the ex-employer.

If a claimant files a claim using somebody else's Social Security number or files against an employer he didn't work for, then the state will prosecute for fraud. Most fraud prosecutions, though, happen when a person files a claim, collects benefits, goes to work, and doesn't report his earned income.

### Can My Benefits Be Garnisheed?

In all states, the unemployment insurance agencies can garnishee benefits for child support, said Peitersen. Some states may garnishee benefits for other reasons, too.

MAINTAINING UNEMPLOYMENT INSURANCE BENEFITS

### What Should I Keep in Mind When Filling Out the Biweekly Claim Cards?

If you qualify for benefits, you will begin receiving your checks within three to four weeks of your filing. A biweekly claim card will probably be attached to the check. In order to receive the next check, you must fill out the card each week, sign it, and mail it.

Generally, the card will ask these questions:

☞ Were you able and available for work? (You can't collect benefits if you were ill or disabled. You must be ready to report to work as you would if you were employed.)

☞ Did you receive severance, vacation or holiday pay, Social Security, or income other than earnings?

☞ Did you attend school or training?

☞ Did you refuse any job offers or separate from any employment?

☞ Did you make a required number of weekly job contacts?

The claim card will ask you if you worked. If so, you must write the name and address of the employer, the number of hours, and the gross earnings. If you did work for which you were not paid that week, you must still write down the hours and estimate how much you would have made had you been paid.

You must also write down the names, addresses, and contacts of the employers you contacted for work. The form also will ask what kind of work you were seeking and what results you had. The state does make random checks, so don't falsify any statements.

Finally, be sure to sign and date the card. Mail it on the day recommended on the card or in your copy of the unemployment insurance handbook.

### How Do I Deal with the Biweekly Filing When I Get Part-time or Temporary Employment?

If you find temporary employment, you're now employed again. You may continue filing the claim cards if you are also sending out résumés and making contacts for other work. However, if the temporary employment will last for a month or more, you may not want to bother with the biweekly claim cards.

Some states stop sending you the cards if their records show that you're working. When you become unemployed again, reopen the claim by visiting or calling the unemployment office. Again, the purpose of taking part-time or temporary work is to stretch out the twenty-six weeks of benefits over fifty-two weeks.

### Should I Declare Proceeds from Selling Personal Possessions?

If you are faced with cashing in securities, collecting charity, or selling off household goods or a car to raise money, that is considered income. But it is not earnings from employment.

Don Peitersen said you have to report *earnings*, not *income*.

## Do I Lose Benefits If I Go to School?

The claim form asks if you've been attending school or training because you can't draw unemployment insurance while you're going to school full-time. In that case, it is assumed that you're not able or available to go to work, and therefore you have dropped out of the labor market.

What you need to answer on the claim form is: Does going to school affect your ability to find work? If you normally work in the daytime from eight to five, for example, you can take a course at night, and that wouldn't affect your ability to report for work. But if you're taking that course from eight to ten in the morning on Mondays, Wednesdays, and Fridays—and it therefore would interfere with your availability for work—you would be denied benefits.

You may qualify for a program to retrain workers called the Job Training Partnership Act (JTPA). This government program enables you to attend school full-time to learn new skills or a new trade.

## HOW TO APPEAL A DISQUALIFICATION

## What Are My Rights If I'm Disqualified for Benefits?

You have the right to appeal any decision that disqualifies you to receive benefits, postpones benefits, or reduces the maximum amount of the benefits you receive. The notice of disqualification will probably provide a form on the back of the page for you to begin the appeals process.

Find out where to call or write to make an appeal, either with that form or with a personal letter. *Be sure to file the appeal by the deadline on the notice of disqualification.*

When you file the appeal, present your facts as they are known to you. The best advice is to be clear and concise. When the state agency gets differing views, it will come back to both parties. It isn't a complicated process. If you are still disqualified after this round of appeals, you may go before a referee of the state's unemployment office.

A person can bring in legal counsel, but the system is designed so you don't need it. Most states want claimants to make a short statement explaining why they want to appeal. This usually takes place at an informal administrative hearing. It is taken under oath and is recorded, but the rules are looser than in court.

The referee will ask you to restate your whole case. The referee's job is to protect both parties, which is why you don't need a lawyer.

The employer and employee come face to face to get it all out for the referee. In order to do the best you can to avoid losing the appeal, remember to:

☞ Prepare and analyze the case and know the issues.
☞ Subpoena any necessary documents or witnesses. File subpoenas early.
☞ Show up on time.
☞ Be prepared to present testimony, documents, and witnesses.
☞ Avoid professional jargon.
☞ Check your emotions and hostility toward your former employer at the door.
☞ Stay rational and calm.

If the referee still turns down your request, you may have other avenues through which to appeal. Your state's unemployment agency probably has booklets or pamphlets to help you through the appeals process.

Regardless of the progress of the appeal, *keep filing your claim cards!*

## TROUBLESHOOTING
### Where Do I Go with Questions?
The first thing to do when you have questions about filing for unemployment insurance, the claim cards, or any other matter is to *read the handbook*. Millions of people have been through this process before you, and the handbooks have been continually revised to deal with and anticipate your questions.

If you can't find an adequate answer in the handbook, visit or call your unemployment insurance office. Don't wait until your benefits stop.

### What Happens If I Go Out of State?
Generally speaking, you can't file a claim while residing in another state. However, if you travel to another state for job-hunting, you can file a courtesy claim from that state. Look in the phone book for the local unemployment office or Job Service. Go there with

your claim card so they can certify your job search activity. They will give you one of their claim cards, which you can fill out and mail to your state.

### What Can I Do If My Benefits Run Out?

If your benefits run out, they run out. After that, you have to find other kinds of assistance. But once your fifty-two-week benefit year expires, you can file for unemployment insurance benefits again.

### What Should I Do If I've Been Overpaid?

Sometimes the state mistakenly overpays you. This may happen because of an error in their calculations or yours, because of your failure to seek work actively while you are drawing benefits, or as the result of pay you received while a decision was under appeal.

If you are overpaid, you must repay. Alternatively, the state will withhold future benefits. Some people ask, "I didn't do anything wrong, and the state just overpaid me. Why can't I keep the money?" But the fact is you received benefits to which you weren't entitled.

### What Should I Do If I'm Called for a Quality Control Review?

The agency routinely and randomly selects names from those who are receiving benefits for a quality control review to determine the accuracy of the benefits payments. If you are selected, you will be notified where and when to appear for an interview. This may be a nuisance, but it shouldn't cause you trouble if you have kept accurate records of your work history, job search, and earnings.

### What Should I Do When I Find a Job?

If you find a job, as you hope you will, you will find yourself in a strange land between unemployment and employment, especially if you don't start working for anywhere from two weeks to a month or more. Often newly hired people can't start work immediately because of family considerations, the need to move to a new job location, conflict with a temporary work obligation, or other reasons.

So you face a dilemma. On one hand, you are technically unemployed until you actually start working. On the other hand, you need to fill out the claim card for your benefits—and those claim cards ask if you are available and able for work, as well as what job contacts you have made that week.

The last issue is dicey. You will rightly feel strange making contacts for jobs you have no intention of taking should they call you. On the other hand, if you don't make job contacts, the state unemployment insurance agency will disqualify you from receiving benefits. So what do you do?

As with any question, first read your unemployment insurance benefits handbook. If that doesn't have a satisfactory answer, call or visit your unemployment insurance office.

Don Peitersen said that some states will ask you to obtain a letter from your new employer stating that you will be going to work for them on a certain date. Depending on the state, either you or your future employer will send this letter to the state unemployment insurance agency and request "job attached" status. You may have the "job contacts" requirements of the claim card forgiven for anywhere from two weeks to however long it will take until you start work for your new employer.

The problem comes in if you live in a state that will forgive that requirement for only two weeks or some specified time that is shorter than the time it will actually take you to start working. You then will still need to make the job contacts, even though you know you must turn them down if they call you. This is admittedly an awkward glitch in the system, but there isn't much you or many state unemployment insurance agencies can do about it.

I suggest that you make contacts for jobs that you know you don't have a chance of getting. However, there's always the possibility that you may find something better than what you already have. Regardless of the outcome, continue to file the claim cards to receive your benefits.

When you start working at your new job, simply stop sending the cards. You don't need to report that you no longer need the benefits.

## JUST STAY CALM

Filing for unemployment insurance benefits will be one of the most tedious experiences you will have during this tough time. If you stay calm, you will be able to look back on it as a minor nuisance. The best way to stay calm is to shelve your emotions about your job loss, read the handbook, and keep accurate records. You are now ready for what may be the long haul of unemployment.

# CHAPTER SEVEN

# Hunkering Down for the Long Haul

S o here it is. Not too long ago you spent your last day at work, cleaned out your desk or locker, said goodbye to your coworkers (if they hadn't been laid off, too) and maybe even to your supervisor as well. You drove home knowing that you'd never drive home along that route again. At supper, you looked at your spouse and children and wondered how long you'd be eating meals like that. Later that night you lay awake in bed, your mind either blank or racing with a thousand questions—but always with the same foreboding sense of "what's next?"

You wake up into a strange new world, contemplating a paradox. On one hand, you're thinking, *I've got nothing to do*—no job to go to. On the other, you're realizing, *I've got everything to do*—to cope with managing your emotions, finances, and family as you look for new employment.

When you were employed, daily life had a way of simply flowing on. You paddled along in the midstream of the working world, not thinking much about preparing for the possibility that the stream might one day leave you high and dry. The bills came in, you paid them, and wondered where the money went. You had the nagging thought, "If I lost my job, I'd be within a month of losing my car, house, or apartment, and I don't know how I'd put food on the table." You buried the questions of what other career possibilities existed, or the thought that it might be a good idea to take some night courses to make yourself more marketable.

But now you've been thrown up on the banks, a fish out of water. That "month" between your last paycheck and destitution is beginning right now. Everything has changed. Those nagging questions and thoughts you used to ignore have just shaken you awake.

How do you react? Does your thinking get sharper, or does your mind just fog up?

## THAT WAS THEN; THIS IS NOW

When unemployment hits, we can fall into one of several traps. We might slip into a false sense of security by assuming that a new job is just around the corner. We might give up in despair and let our circumstances get the best of us. Or we might look for any employment that will keep us solvent, without making the effort to consider what we really want to do.

If our thoughts get cloudy and confused, it could be because we don't deal with crises well. Or we fail to realize what sort of crisis unemployment is. Actually, most crises aren't the sorts of problems that need resolving RIGHT NOW. In fact, frantic reactions will make many crises even worse. For example, if you wreck your car and don't force yourself to remain calm, you may be so intent on repairing the car that you'll accept the first estimate you receive. Instead, if you had taken time to shop around, you might have found a better deal.

The crisis of job loss, like that of a car wreck, is best handled by remaining calm. But even though losing your job may feel like being hit by a car, the crisis is different because of the time element. You know about how long it will take to gather estimates and put the car in the shop for repairs. Insurance hassles or lingering injuries aside, the car wreck crisis will be over at some predictable point, and you will be able to move ahead with your life.

Not so with unemployment. You don't know when it will end. That uncertainty, with such major consequences swinging in the balance, creates its own kind of stress and anxiety.

In my case, I initially felt relieved when I heard I was fired. Once the corporate whip came down, my general attitude began to improve over the few months I had left. A number of people later commented that I began to regain the happiness I had lost more than a year earlier. An editor who was formerly a critic commented that my writing had improved. My personality became more open. My enthusiasm returned because I was sure a new and better job was just around the corner.

At the time, I had a good reason to believe that possibility. A friend of mine was about to resign his job at a newspaper and encouraged me to apply for it. I applied, slogged through a day of interviewing, and soon found out that I was the lead candidate. Even when the paper began looking at other people, I wasn't too worried.

With less than a month left at my job, that optimism sank overnight. My friend called me on his last day at work to tell me that his boss had written the position out of the coming year's budget. "You are the lead candidate for a position that no longer exists," he told me.

I'd grown cocky, sure that I would find another job before my time was through at my paper. With a month left, optimism gave way to panic. I heard that it was far easier to get another job when you were working than when you weren't. I found out how true that was, because I didn't get an offer for another sixteen months.

I never thought I would be out of full-time work for that long. I didn't prepare for it because I didn't think I needed to. That was foolish, and fueled the stress I already felt with losing my job.

DRESS FOR THE STRESS
As you've already found out firsthand, losing a job is a highly stressful experience. Studies have shown that it isn't as hard as the death of a spouse or a child, but it's more difficult than pregnancy and similar to the stress of getting married. And because stressful events seem to run in packs, job loss will compound or cause other stressful situations.

This is why you need a strategy to think clearly about every aspect of your life. Because whether you know it or not, you are going through a process of grieving, complete with the classic stages of denial, rage and anger, bargaining, depression, and finally acceptance.

## Denial
I've heard of people who will deny the reality of being out of work by doing irrational things such as taking vacations after they leave their jobs, partying like there's no tomorrow, embarking on mad shopping sprees, immediately moving out of town, or holing up in their homes to watch soap operas.

Husbands have been known to excel in practicing denial. They've traditionally been the breadwinners for families, so losing their jobs severely damages their male egos. I've known husbands who won't admit that they've been laid off or fired to anyone—including their own children and sometimes even their wives. These men will maintain their working routine by dressing for work and leaving and returning home at the regular times. They spend their days sequestered in a library or coffee shop, imprisoned by shame. Their denial prevents them from taking the kind of action needed to get help or seek new employment.

As corny as it sounds, you need to admit to yourself that you no longer work where you did. You can't go back. Even if your former employer changes his or her mind about letting you go, asks you back, and you return, the situation won't be the same as it was before. Your friendships will change, your financial situation will change, where you live may change, and your career may change. If you don't deal with these issues, they will hinder your job search and your emotional recovery. Give yourself room to react: as with any significant loss, this recognition will very likely cleanse itself with tears.

## Rage and Anger

I'm mostly a peaceable guy. I was never good at contact sports. I think professional wrestling brings out the worst instincts of trumped up emotions.

But I found out just how dark my heart can be when the realization of my unemployment sank in. I wanted to lash out at those who caused this. I wanted to curse, hit, stab, shoot, kill. Sure, I had reared back in horror at the television images of spurned employees who took out their frustrations on their former employers with automatic weapons. But I now could say that I had tasted their rage.

Even more than those horrible thoughts, I wanted to lash out at myself. My angry heart was driven deeper into despair as I found how tempting suicide was. Just end this pain and grief with any one of a number of pharmacological potions or mechanical devices. It would be easy—and selfish and pointless.

So what did I do? I blamed.

Blame it on the stupid bosses. Blame it on my education. Blame it on the company. Blame it on the economy. Blame it on the President, the Congress, the tenured bureaucrats. Blame it on myself. Blame it on God who put me here to begin with. How could they do this to me? How could I do this to myself?

I studied hard. I worked hard. I prayed. I paid my dues. What more does anyone want? This is the American dream we're talking about, right? Do the right things, believe the right things, and you'll make it, right?

But then I welcomed myself to real life. I could blame, hit, and curse what or whomever I wanted. I may have been right, they may have been wrong. They may have been right, and I may have been wrong. We both may have been right—or wrong—for that matter. So what? I could analyze it to death. And what would I get? A corpse—the memory of myself as an employee of a company.

A lot of things don't make sense. Often the most tragic events—personally and publicly—don't have reasons for why they happen. We can't figure out why a loved one walked out on us, why our children sneer at us, why President John F. Kennedy was assassinated, or why we're out of work. The point is that bad things happen. And they don't point a blaming finger at us any more than they point to anyone else.

The point for those of us who are unemployed is that we need to overcome our anger and get on with our lives, regardless of who or what is at fault.

Rage at your former boss won't pay your bills. Anger at the condition of America's economy—or Japan's or Europe's economies for that matter—won't get you another job. Ceaseless questions about "why did God allow this to happen?" won't help you retool your skills to become self-empowered for another career. And harboring fantasies of violence will do nothing for—and in fact will prove harmful to—your ability to relate to family, friends, prospective employers, and most of all yourself.

It's okay to be angry. Anger lets you know that something isn't right, that there are matters of justice in urgent need of resolution. But nursing anger without channeling it constructively will lock you into a perpetual state of wanting revenge, rather that actually resolving your unemployment. Once you get over the anger and learn to cope with the stresses of the everyday life of unemployment with its bargaining and depression, you can move toward the acceptance of a new life and a new career.

## THE LONG HAUL THROUGH UNEMPLOYMENT

The challenge for those of us who are unemployed—or for those who know someone who is unemployed—is to turn anger into assets. You don't have a steady income or security now that you're unemployed.

But believe it or not, you have one very crucial asset unavailable to those who are working: time.

This asset of time will give you an opportunity to restructure and reassess your life. It can give you the opportunity to understand your self-worth, improve your relationships with family and friends, hone your financial planning, take a look at your career, and retool your job skills.

My seventeen months of unemployment was the most worthwhile experience of my life. But unlike worthwhile experiences of travel, education, romance, or marriage, unemployment is an experience I would never wish upon anyone else. Yet having that asset of time, I learned how to prepare for the future in ways that would never have occurred to me otherwise.

Even if you've been out of work for months already, there are some practical things you can do to help you hunker down for what could be a long haul. They start with rethinking your self-esteem, taking care of yourself and your family, learning to be more resourceful and careful in the marketplace, resisting temptations and employment scams, considering part-time or temporary work, and coping when you think you're at the end of your rope.

You have a new job now. It's called unemployment. You need to approach it as diligently as you approached your old job. You had your old job for quite a while. You may find out the hard way that you will have your new job for a long time, too.

More than anything else, you must remember that you are a person of worth. You are more valuable than any job. And your worth has nothing to do with job, title, position, or lack thereof.

# II

◆◆

# "How Am I Going to Make It?"

—

# Surviving Day by Day

# CHAPTER EIGHT

# Renewing Your Self-Esteem

T hink of the people you've known, including yourself, who have lost their jobs. After the initial shock (or even relief) wore off, how did they react? Did they carry themselves well, order their lives, and embark on a job search? Or did they withdraw, feel worthless, and sink into despair?

What makes the difference between these two kinds of reactions? I experienced both of them myself. I think the crucial ingredient is not so much the specific factors of job loss as it is how we deal with our self-esteem.

ELVIS AND ME

Several months after I left the newspaper, job prospects were vanishing as steadily as each week's help wanted classifieds landed in the trash. Winter faded into spring. Friendships withered through neglect or my shame and inattention. Job hunting seemed pointless.

My ability to explain myself faltered. I withdrew. I wanted to live like the mythical Elvis: drugged, elusive, and known for making random appearances at mundane places like gas stations, convenience stores, and shopping malls.

Unemployment can make even the most gregarious souls want to play possum. How do you explain your situation? How can you wish others Merry Christmas or Happy Fourth of July when all you can muster is a plastic mask with a manufactured smile?

It's embarrassing. It's humiliating. That stubborn stigma of shame won't go away. Even when others are understanding, you feel as if you don't deserve any sympathy. You're willing and certainly eager to go to work as a contributing member of society. You have always done your part to drop a check in the collection plate, donate your time when your help is needed, and pitch in for community food and clothing drives.

But now you're stuck. You sense a wide gap between who you think you are and who you'd like to be. You feel financially paralyzed because you can't contribute, and now you may even be on the receiving end of charity. It seems so degrading. How could it happen that you've joined those poor souls standing in line for free Christmas presents or shopping for second-hand clothing at the thrift shop? Standing in the unemployment line was for those other people, unfortunate or dumb enough to get trapped in a declining industry when they should have known better.

You avoid eye contact. You don't feel cheerful when the clerk hands you the grocery receipt and says "have a nice day." The clerk is having a nicer day than you are.

Yet as hard as this is, it's just as difficult when your family tries to cover up for you or doesn't know what to say. My parents wouldn't tell their friends how their number-one son was doing, other than to say he was living and working out West. One friend whose cousin was recently laid off from an upper-management position told me that she hadn't called him because she simply didn't know what to say.

How do you put a constructive spin on unemployment? In many ways you can't, without sounding like Pollyanna. You now learn first-hand what nonsense it is when well-meaning friends tell others that you're "seeking new opportunities" or "exploring career options." Unemployment dulls your senses and smashes your ego flat. But unemployment can do at least one good thing: it can force you to confront who you are.

## BROKEN GLASS, WOUNDED EGOS

Attaining and maintaining strong self-esteem is not a matter of "feeling good" about yourself. You can buy all sorts of potions—legal or illegal—designed to make you feel good for a while. But they aren't going to do much for your self-esteem.

The foundations of self-esteem are laid during our infancy by the nurturing styles of our parents or guardians. If they nurtured us well, they loved us unconditionally even when they chastised us for our mistakes. Ideally, the lesson we should have learned is that we're loved regardless of what we do. Sadly, it doesn't always turn out that way.

As adults, we revise or gain a healthy self-esteem from a sober, deep personal knowledge that we are valuable, regardless of what we do. It sounds simple, but that knowledge doesn't come easily. Sometimes it's earned through extraordinary struggle and even horrifying experiences.

I once interviewed a Jewish woman who lived through Kristallnacht, the "night of broken glass," in Nazi Germany on November 9, 1938. Kristallnacht was the Nazi-led pogrom carried out by storm troopers who smashed windows, destroyed shops, murdered or arrested Jews, and torched synagogues. It prefigured the Holocaust to come. This woman's father owned and operated a perfume shop in Cologne. The storm troopers—many of whom were neighbors—destroyed her father's shop. They broke down the door, tipped over counters and shelves, and smashed hundreds of bottles of perfumes.

This woman's life changed overnight. She learned who her friends were—and who they weren't. In the following months, she was separated from her family, moved out of the country, and began a new education and a new life. She had no choice if she wanted to live. The lessons took hold fast and hard. Fifty years later, this woman said that for all its terror, Kristallnacht had taught her a lifetime lesson: "I have no identity crisis, and never have had one."

Through this horrifying experience, she found something that has eluded many others. She quickly learned who she was in order to rise above that tragedy.

Although not as horrifying, unemployment can also shake us into an understanding of our self-worth. The thing that so many of us looked to as the source of our self-worth, our job, is gone. It's often during crisis situations when we grow up. Through no desire of our own, we've been brought to this point. The question before us is, how are we going to cope with it?

We start with the pain. Pain isn't all bad. It can let us know that we have a wound in need of diagnosis and healing. That doesn't mean that correcting our understanding or even developing a healthy self-esteem will make all the pain disappear. But by paying attention to what the pain is telling us, we can learn how to cope with loss. We can acquire the inner strength to carry on. We can see things in appropriate perspective.

A solid sense of self-worth will also go far to protect us from vulnerability to our personal weakness or the predatory designs of others (see chapters 12 and 13). It gives us a solid base for learning how to conduct a job hunt based on who we are and what we have to offer rather than on playing the lottery of reading help-wanted ads.

Sure, you can find new work without dealing with your self-worth. But why not take the very real pain you feel and wrestle with these issues now so you will be stronger for the struggles ahead—including the struggles after you find work?

## SO WHO ARE YOU, ANYWAY?

Work lies at the center of our personal lives, our families, and our culture. Many common names—Smith, Cooper, Miller, Farmer—were given centuries ago to people because of what they did. At parties, church, or on the subway, the most frequent and probing question still is, "What do you do?"

The answer to that question nails down more than what your schedule is from eight to five. It opens up insights into your social class, what kind of house or apartment you live in, what model of car you drive, your family, your neighborhood, your education, possibly your religion, and your friends. It lets the questioner know whether he or she has anything in common with you, and if so, how much. "What do you do?" not only opens the door to job or business contacts, but also to new social relationships.

"What do you do?" is not a bad question—unless you don't have an answer. Responding "I'm out of work" or even "I'm between jobs" does more than sidestep the secondary questions about class, lifestyle, neighborhood, education, religion, family, and friends. "Unemployed" often implies that you're a nobody. Even worse than being a nobody, you may be considered a parasite on society because you may be drawing on unemployment benefits, food stamps, and charity resources. The status implies that you're not pulling your own weight, that you're headed for financial and social problems. And nobody wants to hang around trouble.

Who are you, anyway? You already knew before you were unemployed that you were more than your job, more than what you did, more than what you may have spent years training to do.

Before you were unemployed, you spent more than two-thirds of your time away from work. You already had a life of family, friends, social involvement, activities, trips. If you married, it probably wasn't on the basis of what your spouse did for a living.

But your work wasn't just a peripheral commitment next to whatever you did with the other two-thirds of your life. Your job enabled you to earn the money that paid the bills for all those activities. More importantly, it may have been an expression of your creativity and aspirations.

You probably disliked some aspects of your job. You may even have even hated it. But you drew some identification from it nonetheless. That's because your work is an extension of something very deep within yourself, although it's not who you are. The key to making this distinction—and gaining a healthy self-esteem—lies with understanding the origin of your self-worth.

## GOD MADE ME, AND GOD DOESN'T MAKE JUNK

You've probably learned that a healthy self-esteem is not achieved by getting others to flatter you. The problem with flattery, of course, is that it's never enough. Flattery never helps you realize that self-worth is built into who you are, not something you earn by what you do. Self-worth starts with something much greater than that.

Many religions teach that we are created in God's image. That's not saying we *are* God, but that our worth is greater than anything else God made. God made us, and God doesn't make junk. Our dignity comes from the belief that God gave us bodies, intellects, emotions, and aspirations. These gifts enable us to create and love. God loves us, even when we can't emotionally respond to it, or when circumstances seem to militate against it.

But make no mistake—we aren't perfect, either. In a perfect world, there wouldn't be layoffs, firings, "downsizings," personality conflicts, or recessions. Our emotions aren't innocent, either. We know all too well the rage at our former employers or the economy. This anger is not constructive: it changes little or nothing and leaves us paralyzed. We've known the darkness in our hearts as we mentally rage against those who hurt us, as we long for the temporary comfort of illicit relationships, or even as we struggle against fantasies of our own self-destruction.

These emotions and fantasies tear at our own worth and others'.

They undermine our dignity and feed on increasingly dark desires with ever more unsatisfying results. They don't satisfy us because they run counter to and away from what we were made to be: valuable persons who create because we are created in God's image.

Many of the world's major religions teach that we are valuable because God made us that way. The moral codes of these religions were designed to steer us away from actions that embrace evil and diminish our value. The struggle between good and evil occupies center stage in the drama of human history. Likewise, our personal dramas often turn on how we understand our worth. This personal worth is spelled out in the opening pages of the Bible:

> God said, "Let us make man in our image, in our likeness, and
> let them rule over the fish of the sea and the birds of the air,
> over the livestock, over all the earth, and over all the creatures
> that move along the ground."
> So God created man in his own image,
>     in the image of God he created him;
>     male and female he created them.

That's pretty heady stuff. This passage asserts that we have more value than any other created being.

Other passages throughout the Hebrew and Christian Bibles repeat this same theme. King David wrote:

> What is man that you are mindful of him,
>     the son of man that you care for him?
> You made him a little lower than the heavenly beings
>     and crowned him with glory and honor. (Psalm 8)

David, the greatest military and political leader in Israel's history, could motivate people because he honored their value. He wrote elsewhere in this psalm that God gave them the privilege to manage the rest of creation.

In the Sermon on the Mount, Jesus told his followers not to worry about the future, because they had great self-worth and everything was in God's hands. For example, Jesus told them, "Look at the birds of the air; they do not sow or reap or store away in barns, and yet your heavenly Father feeds them. Are you not much more valuable than they?"

Other religions, such as Islam, echo a similar theme: We are made in the image of God: therefore, we're valuable. We're the crown of creation, not a sideshow.

We express that value in a variety of ways, but most of all in our work. No doubt a lot of jobs are crummy, boring, and downright dangerous. I've worked at some of them. But even the rotten jobs let me know that work is ideally something more than screwing nut A on bolt B at Amalgamated Widget Inc.

The kind of work we know we are created for lets us plan, create, design, build, account, modify, renovate, restore, and decorate. We sing about it, cry about it, write about it, paint it, and sculpt it. In other words, we express how we are created in the image of God when we work. We have an integral part in this whole grand scheme of things. This is programmed into us, just like the biological imperatives to eat, sleep, and procreate.

That programming gets its circuits blown when we lose our jobs. The anguish and loss of self-esteem we feel are closely connected to our human nature. The secret to maintaining our self-esteem is to realize that our desire to work existed long before our jobs ever came along. The love God has for us continues regardless of whether or not we're employed. The value that we have within ourselves—including this desire to work—is more important than any job.

## LET'S GET PRACTICAL

No other person can give you a healthy self-esteem. Counselors, psychologists, and psychiatrists can't do it, no matter how much you pay them. They can only guide you by asking questions, coax you to accept it, and get you to understand it yourself.

Grasping our self-worth requires struggle. The effort is hard, but the reward is great.

The following questions provide some exercises for helping you develop your self-esteem. Get paper and pencil. Answer these questions honestly. Meditate and refine your responses. They will come in handy when you start down the road to employment in the last section of the book.

1. Do I love or feel good about myself? Why or why not?
2. What can I do to take care of myself right now?

3. Do I love others?
4. What can I do to love others more?
5. What do I like about my body, my face?
6. What are my strengths and weaknesses?
7. How can I use my strengths more effectively?
8. How can I turn my weaknesses into strengths?
9. What are three problems I've faced in the past month, and how have I solved them?
10. How can I apply those solutions to my unemployment?

In the next chapter you will explore some ways in which you can apply problem-solving experiences to your unemployment. They include volunteering, self-education, exercise, celebrations, and humor. But you also can apply the contents of this chapter to the moments— sometimes long moments—when unemployment seems to drape over you like a shroud.

## You Are Not Alone

Think about your personal heroes who have overcome seemingly impossible odds to triumph in their field. Every line of work and every field of interest has them: athletes, engineers, doctors, soldiers, construction workers, scholars, people in religious vocations, tradespeople, politicians, musicians, artists, business people, teachers, government employees. The individual stories are different. The themes are not. You share in these same themes.

If you probe, you will find that these individuals challenged and conquered physical disabilities, the ridicule of their peers, the oppression of tyrants, or the dark night of the soul. You will find their struggles have much in common with yours. Although no one has traveled your road, others have traveled similar paths and found fulfillment.

Great literature embodies the universal nature of this journey in its portrayal of drama, conflict, heartache, triumph, and joy. That's why works as diverse as the Bible, J.R.R. Tolkien's *The Lord of the Rings,* and the writings of the Rev. Martin Luther King, Jr., have such staying power. They convey in a deep and true way how characters, real or fictitious, have responded to something profound when they could have sat on the sidelines of life. As you reflect on lives and literature, you will come to see that self-worth has been an issue since the beginning of time, and will continue as long as the human race exists.

## Letting Go

One of the best opportunities for building your self-esteem is to learn how to let go of your past, especially your past employment. This hinges on forgiveness. It's hard.

The causes of unemployment can be very big or very small. Regardless of the particular configuration of circumstances, which can be as varied as the number of companies and employees, anger is a common element. Whatever the reasons for your joblessness, they can easily breed resentment and bitterness. They will eat you alive if you let them. But letting go of them is no easy task. After all, it's the word of your dismissal that rings daily in your ears. You are reminded of it every time you send out a résumé and every time you forgo a little luxury such as a first-run movie.

Even harder than forgetting is forgiving those who wronged you. They include corporate executives more concerned about their status than the welfare of the employees who helped put them there. They also include supervisors who admitted to you that they didn't know what your job was about, and then gave you assignments that proved it.

The problem with hanging on to these memories is that you give them power over you when you nurse them. You don't respond with the strength that you find in your self-worth. Instead, you react defensively by fantasizing about revenge. The more you dwell on your angry desire to get back at them, the less control you take over your own life.

As trite as it may sound, the only way out is to forgive and forget. Renewed self-esteem works hand in hand with forgiveness. As you realize that you are valuable, and flawed as well, you also know that those who have harmed you are valuable, and flawed as well. Regardless of what they did, they have their lives to live. You have your life to live, too. You can go your separate way only as much as you are mentally and spiritually able to forgive them, wish them well, and then head down your own road.

## Hanging On

Renewing your self-esteem won't happen by chanting an "I am valuable" mantra. It will happen as you apply the genuine understanding of who you are to the daily tasks you must accomplish to keep your sanity. For example, as the rejection letters come in (given that the prospective employers care enough to write back), you may need to remind yourself continually that they are not telling you that you're no good. You may just need to say that the needs of the prospective firm couldn't match the skills you had to offer.

As the savings account withers, you may need to remind yourself that you will be provided for. You won't starve. You will have a place to sleep. You will have clothes to wear.

And as your spouse and children wonder when they will be able to live a "normal" life again, you may need to remind them that you have each other. You may need to remind them that surviving unemployment involves more than just you trying to find a job. It concerns how all of you will rise above the circumstances in ways you may not be able to recognize now. The love of family or friends will keep you strong even when it all looks bleak.

This isn't easy. But you've made it so far, right? You will find courage. You will make it. You will find hands reaching out to grab yours, even when your hold seems certain to slip. Say a prayer, give your loved ones a hug, and hang on.

APPLYING SELF-WORTH
Self-worth is more than an abstract concept. It is power. We're not just creatures of habit or fate. We possess the ability to rise above our circumstances. Being unemployed is not an excuse to cave in to the fatalism of "I can't do anything." In the following chapters, we will learn what we can do for ourselves and our families during our unemployment.

CHAPTER NINE

# Take Good Care of Yourself

❖

S o here it is, another day of unemployment. Another day, another . . .
day. No dollars here.

Another excuse to sleep in until 10:30 a.m., right? No way. Just
because you're out of work doesn't mean it's party time, at least if you
have any desire to maintain your personal dignity or find a job.

Sure, it's easy to let personal care slip when you face a crisis,
especially job loss. You have a lot of time, which can be an enemy or
a friend. What will you do with it all?

You will spend a lot of time figuring out what you want to do and
looking for a job. But you also have a house or apartment to care for, not
to mention family and friends. And you have yourself to take care of,
too. Acting on your self-esteem means taking care of yourself—spiritually, physically, mentally, and more. If you don't take care of yourself,
it's going to be much harder for you to keep pace with the job hunt and
take care of those you love. (Although the suggestions in this chapter
are appropriate for anyone who is out of work, they are especially applicable to single persons who may not have the networks that married
persons have. See chapter 10 for suggestions that are especially applicable to unemployed persons who are taking care of a family.)

LET US RISE
During my unemployment, there were many days when I simply wanted
to withdraw. Even making phone calls was daunting, because I felt less
than cheerful. Sometimes I felt downright rotten.

How do you take care of yourself when it feels as if there's not a whole lot to care about?

The secret is found in part in an old-fashioned word *deportment,* which means "the manner of conducting or bearing oneself." You get up in the morning, groom yourself, hold your head up, look people in the eye, smile, say "please" and "thank you." Sounds trite, doesn't it? Yet this is more than Etiquette 101. It's critical to how you will maintain your dignity in otherwise less-than-dignified circumstances.

Although these components of deportment are essential to the job hunt, they are even more essential to your own self-respect. You can't insist that others respect you if you don't respect yourself. Be assertive. Maintain at least the appearance of knowing where you're going. You are created in God's image—why not act like it?

## LET US PRAY

They say there are no atheists in foxholes. There aren't too many atheists in classrooms, either. Most students who haven't studied will toss a prayer to heaven before they take a test, regardless of Supreme Court decisions about prayer in public schools. And there probably aren't many atheists standing in unemployment lines.

No matter what your religious background may be, you probably came face to face with your own limitations when you realized that your job was fading into history. Where do you turn when all your efforts fail? I faced this foxhole issue when I knew my days at my former job were numbered.

As circumstances were coming to a head, I asked my editor to meet me in the conference room. What began as an outburst of anger with my job and a desire to leave it turned into an hour-long argument. The more I pressed my points, the more desperate I became. What had started as a venting of frustrations ended as a lost battle. Frightened of what I had initiated, I drove home, sat on my bed, and broke down. I didn't know what would happen next, but I knew that my days at the newspaper were numbered.

I can't recall any other time in my life when I cried so hard. Lungs and stomach expelled anguish and anger as I wailed, "God, does anybody want me?" My tears soaked my pillow, my breathing grew less labored, and my sobs gave way to sleep.

What else besides prayer is there at a time like that? No one else is listening. No one else *can* listen. Prayer—communication with

God—fills in the void of our sorrow. In the most painful moments of our lives, we realize that our relationship with our Creator is the best thing we have.

At times such as these, however, it's easy to forget what else we have. We are the same people we were before we lost our jobs. We have the same talents, skills, and desires. We have the same place to live. We have the same friends and family who care for us more than we know. This is more than mere happiness. And it isn't denying our pain, either.

When you're pressed by the squeeze plays of life, give in to the impulse to pray. And count your blessings. That form of thanksgiving will ease the darkness of the loss you feel, or at least shed a little light to put it in perspective.

Many, many people have found that when they pray and count their blessings, they also find help to order their lives and begin to build a new career. Building that new world, with God's help, involves deliberately structuring your days and weeks.

## LIFE GOES ON: DEVELOPING A ROUTINE

Two hours after I cried myself to sleep, I woke up to learn the first lesson of unemployment: *Life goes on.* Regardless of what I was feeling, my emotions had to yield to my other responsibilities. I washed my face, changed clothes, and drove to the local university where I had to teach my first class of that term. I felt miserable, but that was quite irrelevant to my students.

Don't wallow in your job loss. At the least, it will cripple your soul. At worst, you will open yourself to some dangerous temptations and scams. Instead, consciously map out your hours, days, and weeks to weather the storms and doldrums of unemployment.

You will find that your energy level and your schedules will fluctuate. But developing and maintaining a routine is essential for your emotional well-being and your efficiency in the job hunt.

There will be days when you don't even want to get out of bed. You will want nothing more than to pull the covers over your head and wish it would all go away. I often wondered what was the point of going through the motions of being active, even when I had résumés to send out and odd jobs to do. But I learned that I had to set my feelings aside and get moving. A new day was here, and there was nothing I could do to hold it back.

Your job now is to begin looking for new work. In all likelihood, you won't find it immediately. So try keeping a routine:

☞ Get up each morning as if you had a job. Shower, eat breakfast, dress appropriately, and carry yourself as though you have a purpose—because you do.

☞ Be at your desk, at the coffee shop to meet contacts, or at the library at a regular time as if you were still working.

☞ Keep your personal work area free of clutter.

☞ If you have children at home, as much as possible set aside periods of time in which you clearly establish that Daddy or Mommy is working hard to find a new job or is concentrating on personal projects, so you should not be disturbed during those periods except in emergencies.

☞ Track your time and accomplishments with a daily notebook.

☞ Track your emotional development with a journal or diary. For the first week or two, you may find it helpful to write down everything you can recall about what happened with your former employer, analyzing both what they did and what you did. (This will also be useful later when you work on focusing, write a résumé, and prepare for your interview, as we'll see in chapters 16-19.)

☞ List job contacts in your unemployment insurance handbook (provided by the state's unemployment insurance agency).

☞ Eat dinner with your family. Spend time with your children. Maintain intimacy with your spouse.

☞ Spend time with your boyfriend, girlfriend, or fiancé.

☞ Spend time with your friends.

☞ Go to bed at a decent hour so you get enough sleep.

You will have days when you fail. You will sleep in, get depressed, curl up in a fetal position on the couch, eat junk food, and watch television. Don't worry about it. Give yourself room to "fail." But acknowledge to yourself that you took the easy escape, and go to bed resolving that tomorrow will be better. *Just don't give up.*

WHEN DEPRESSION CLOSES IN
Despite your best efforts at taking care of yourself, you may be afflicted by depression. Job loss and unemployment are traumatic enough to trigger

depression. And if unemployment continues long enough, battling depression will consume an immense amount of energy.

Especially if you have had a personal or family history of depression, you need to take extra care of yourself when despair sets in. Depression can slow you down, stop you in your tracks, or send you to the hospital. Here are some of the basic warning signs:

☞ Profound and unending sadness.

☞ Difficulty sleeping.

☞ Desire to sleep during the day.

☞ Inability to focus on tasks.

☞ Feelings of hopelessness and/or loss.

☞ Feelings of failure.

☞ Frequent illnesses. Many people have said that they became prone to illness during their unemployment. It's a symptom of the depression and the stress that come with the territory. Illness is further complicated when you either lose health benefits or must pay cash for health care, further cutting into your scarce resources.

☞ Erratic eating patterns.

☞ Loss of sexual desire.

☞ Suicidal thoughts. This is critical. If you have entertained notions of ending your life, see a doctor and/or psychiatrist *now*. These tendencies are not normal. Acting on suicidal impulses will end *your* problems, but it will create a devastating new set of problems that will crush those who love and care for you. *Never take suicidal temptations lightly.*

Maintaining a daily routine, adequate sleep, exercise, and personal relationships will go far to thwart depression. But if symptoms persist, do not hesitate to seek professional help. Contact your local mental health association or religious congregation for help or referrals.

NAME THAT INSULT

When your self-esteem is on the rocks—especially during unemployment—you are even more vulnerable to wounding by those who pick at you for your faults. Parents, spouses, coworkers, and friends may try to make light of your unemployment—in well-meaning, clumsy, or just plain vicious ways. They may hurl insensitive or tacky comments, insults, or even a sarcastic laugh over the fact that you've lost your job.

You may not be able to do much to keep others from saying unkind things to you. But you *can* do something about how you're going to handle them.

These are examples of insults and insensitive comments I and unemployed friends have heard:

☞ "Haven't you gotten a job *yet*?"

☞ "It will turn out for the best." (This rings hollow if the person saying it has a job and income and you don't.)

☞ "It's easier on you because you're single."

☞ "It's easier on you because you're married."

☞ "God meant it for your good."

☞ "Things could be worse."

☞ "Well, if you were more conscientious [or hadn't been so proud] you wouldn't be in this position."

When you're on the receiving end of comments like these, just smile and let it go. If others persist, tell them they wouldn't say that to someone whose loved one had just died. Then just walk away.

WHAT ELSE YOU CAN DO

Let's assume that now you've developed a routine. You're diligent and industrious. This week alone you mailed twenty résumés, made thirty phone calls, and read three rejection letters (even though you were expecting at least ten times that many responses considering all the résumés you've sent out in the past month). Now what?

Here are other ways to take care of yourself. They seem mundane, but they will help take your mind off unemployment while reminding you that you are a valuable person.

**Volunteer**

Since you're not able to give money to charity, why not give your time by tutoring, teaching, working at a soup kitchen, reading to hospital patients or children at a library, or coaching a sport? Not only will you help others, you will build a healthy self-esteem by showing yourself that you can contribute to society.

## Educate Yourself

Read a book. Attend lectures at local colleges, universities, churches, or synagogues. If you can swing the finances and avoid jeopardizing your unemployment insurance benefits, take a night class at a local community college. Look for job retraining seminars and classes.

## Take up a Hobby

Reacquaint yourself with a hobby or an avocation that you've neglected in recent years—if it doesn't take time away from the job search and if it doesn't cost money.

## Go on a Personal Retreat

Many churches and religious orders offer programs in which you can go on spiritual retreats for a nominal fee. Do this only if you can afford it and if it won't interfere with job hunting or family concerns.

## Find a Support Group

Your church, local community college, YMCA, or other civic organizations may have job support groups. However, beware of groups in which people simply badmouth their former employers and bemoan the state of the job market. You already know that you got a bum deal and that jobs are hard to find. What you need are people who can guide you to better self-acceptance, perhaps offer charity, give suggestions on developing a focus, and help you with résumé-writing, networking, and interviewing skills. (See part 3 for more information on these issues.)

## Exercise

Exercise is one of the best and cheapest ways you have to work off stress and anger in your current situation. You will find you're more alert, and you'll stay healthier.

"It makes you feel good about yourself," said one woman executive who was fired from her job. She asks people to join her as she rides her bike or does aerobics, and stays in touch with people as a result. "You've got to keep going. You have to force yourself. You have a hundred and one excuses why you shouldn't exercise. But if I didn't do it, I'd be one grouchy lady. I recharge my batteries. I get on a high, and I'm not swallowed up by negatives constantly."

There are many ways to exercise, from calisthenics at home (with workout videos or exercise programs on television), to walking or running through city parks, to exercise clubs at schools or city programs. Use your imagination—but more importantly, use your body.

## Eat Healthy

If you shop carefully, it won't cost you any more to eat well than to eat poorly. Cooking doesn't have to be time-consuming and elaborate, either. (And besides, as any unemployed person can tell you, you have time, so why not use that time to refresh yourself on the basics of healthy cooking?)

The primary benefit of eating well is that your health will be better, which will reduce medical expenses. You also won't be as physically drained by the massive amounts of sugar, fat, and sodium loaded into fast foods.

## Celebrate

Celebrations, parties, and holidays are windows into life as we wish it could be all the time. You might even say they're glimpses of heaven. Unemployment is something we don't want, and so celebrations become that much more important.

I've learned to light candles for dinner even when I eat alone, play more music at home, and further refine my sense of humor. This isn't a way of covering the pain of unemployment. The pain is still there. But private and family celebrations and gatherings with friends let you know that you are more than just an economic entity.

## HUMOR: SUPERMAN'S PAL JIMMY OLSEN AND ME

Humor is one of the greatest gifts we have. It lets us know that we truly are human. Our aspirations, desires, and dignity are God-given. They are also limited. Humor helps us celebrate who we really are by enabling us to recognize our limitations without being overcome by them.

Humor helped me laugh at my limitations as it hit home that I wasn't about to land a reporting job anytime soon. The year of my unemployment was one of the worst years in the history of the American newspaper industry. Financial statistics of publicly traded newspaper companies were headed primarily in one direction: down. Prospective employer after prospective employer kept telling me, "Your clips and résumé are impressive, but we have a hiring freeze" . . . ad nauseam.

But I had no idea how bad real life journalism was until I read that fantasy journalism was even worse off. "Jimmy Olsen Loses Job at Daily Planet," stated the headline of the 25 May 1991 issue of *Editor & Publisher* (the trade journal of the newspaper business). No lie! Here's America's best-known cub reporter at Metropolis' premier paper, and Superman's best pal to boot, losing his job in a tight newspaper market. According to *Editor & Publisher,* Michael Carlin (*Superman* editor) reported that "Olsen's future holds many odd jobs, some of them pretty demeaning. Clark Kent, a.k.a. Superman, and Lois Lane will not join Olsen in the unemployment lines."

Just to keep my unemployment situation in perspective, I photo-copied that page of bad news. I circled the article and wrote, "You know getting a job in journalism is tough when . . ." with an arrow pointing to the headline. Then I taped the photocopy to my refrigerator.

I felt bad for Jimmy Olsen, real bad. But somehow, I didn't feel quite so bad for myself.

# CHAPTER TEN

# Take Good Care of Your Family

S teve, a married father of three girls, lost his accounting job in Virginia when his wife was pregnant with their fourth child. He had always believed that his company would take care of him. He lost that religion overnight. "One day things are rosy. Then all of a sudden all these things you've been counting on are gone," he said. "You have the rug pulled out from under you and you are gasping for air."

Steve and his family struggled, but he found that he could farm out his accounting skills in part-time jobs. He and Barb cut back all possible expenses with minimal disruption of family life. After fourteen months, Steve found work. Through it all, he learned some valuable tips—from finances to food to fun—for navigating families through the rough seas of unemployment.

Steve's and Barb's experiences may be similar to your own. Yet no two families are alike—ranging from single parents, to married couples with or without children, to families with more than two generations living at home, to as many different environments as there are individuals. Regardless of the particular family structure, any one family member's unemployment affects how the entire family functions.

Does this mean that family members are worse off than single persons when unemployment strikes? Yes it does. And no it doesn't.

WHO IS BETTER OFF DURING UNEMPLOYMENT—
SINGLES OR FAMILY MEMBERS?
It's just plain human to think that the grass is always greener on the

other side of the fence. When we compare our unemployed status with others' circumstances of unemployment, we're likely to think that those in different marital states are somehow better off than we are. The problem with this attitude is much deeper than economics. The issue is jealousy, which can lead us into making bad decisions based on envious feelings.

For example, let's say your marriage is shaky. When you lose your job, it inflames tensions at home. You may look at individuals who are single and assume that they don't have as many problems as you do. This assumption subconsciously undermines your marriage.

On the other hand, let's say you're single. Your unemployment exacerbates any feelings you may already have about being lonely, poor, or financially vulnerable. Because of these aggravated feelings, you might rush into an engagement or marriage when you aren't ready.

Singles have their own struggles. And so do families. Neither group has the advantage—or the disadvantage—over the other in the leveling effects of unemployment. But that doesn't mean that there aren't some general distinctions between the two groups that are helpful to recognize.

### The Advantages of Being Single

If you are single, you do have some advantages. They include:

*Mobility.* You can move yourself much easier than if you have a family to move as well, not to mention whether your spouse should quit his or her job to move.

*Job hunting.* Your geographical range in looking for new employment may not be restricted as it might be if a spouse is employed and wants to stay at his or her job.

*Freedom from family concerns.* You don't have to worry about feeding, clothing, transporting, and sheltering children or spouse during your unemployment.

But along with the advantages of being single comes a major disadvantage: loneliness, in the absence of spouse and children who will love and encourage you. This loneliness can open you to avenues of seeking comfort through substance abuse or promiscuity. Many singles—for the very fact that they probably aren't responsible to members of an immediate family—don't push as hard to find new work. Nor do many of them budget their money as closely as those who are married and/or care for families. And of course, they don't have the extra income from a working spouse.

## The Advantages of Being Married
If you are married, you have advantages, too. They include:

☞ A close network of people who love you.
☞ An added source (or potential source) of income.
☞ The opportunity to share experiences of struggle and triumph that are routine during unemployment.
☞ The added push from others to find new work.

The disadvantages of marriage and/or children include reduced mobility and worry about caring for others besides yourself.

Neither marital condition is more "suited" to unemployment. Unemployment is hard on everyone. (The major exception to this rule is the struggles faced by single parents. They have few of the advantages and all of the disadvantages of singles and married couples.) So rejoice in whatever marital status you have. Be content and happy. Make adjustments where necessary. Socialize with those in different marital situations and realize that they have their struggles, too. You may find that you can offer suggestions and support for each other.

Following are several families' accounts about how they coped with their unemployment.

NUCLEAR FAMILIES
Steve and Barb had never really considered the possibility that he'd lose his job. "I had the typical attitude of thinking that if somebody lost his job, he deserved it for some reason," Steve recalled. "I was calloused to people going through this."

Steve said that despite the shock of being out the door the same afternoon, he got a pretty good deal from his company. He received a severance package based on his years of service with the company. With that money, he paid off his car loan and eliminated the family's consumer debt. This positioned them well with creditors for the uncertain times ahead.

A lot of people don't fare as well, he added, but that still didn't take the edge off the pain. "I found it very depressing to be with all the other people out of work. I felt like I was in a leper colony."

Over Barb's objections of "We don't take government handouts," Steve filed for unemployment insurance benefits. "I didn't think there was any shame in that," he said, because his ex-employer had contributed to his state's unemployment insurance program.

Steve and Barb had always been frugal, so they didn't have much to cut out. Steve made a budget to determine the minimum income necessary to live on. "That was a good guide for what I could take in lower-paying jobs," he explained. They stuck to the basics and cut out the soft drinks, junk food, cable television, and magazine subscription renewals. "We kept the heat as low as we could stand. In summer we kept the air conditioning as low as we could." Although they never missed a house payment, Steve and Barb realized they should have contacted their mortgage company early in his unemployment.

Steve and Barb had always enjoyed a strong marriage, and Steve's unemployment strengthened it. Barb, however, got tired of Steve hanging around the house. She believed that the wife should stay at home while the husband worked. But unemployment changed that attitude. Barb took in sewing projects and even did cleaning for the neighbors, which was a blow to her upper-middle-class sensibilities. While she was working outside the home, Steve chipped in more with the household tasks and caring for the children. "We had our emotional ups and downs," Steve said. "But we were never at the point where we said, 'We can't go on with this anymore.'"

Unemployment never appeared to affect their young children, but their seven-year-old caught on to what was happening. "When we were planning on doing something," Steve recalled, "the oldest would say, 'Do we need to spend money on that?'"

Steve found that his most frustrating experience centered on finding a new job—at least one that paid what he made before his layoff. Most of the people he worked for part-time understood his predicament and gave him time to look for a permanent position. He did tax work, consulting, and part-time accounting jobs.

Steve considers himself fortunate to have worked part-time for six of the fourteen months of his unemployment, but he learned humility in the process. One time, a friend hired him to count traffic for a day. "There were two of us with master's degrees sitting at an intersection counting cars," Steve wryly remembered.

He finally took an accounting position for a lower salary than what he had earned before, and family life returned to normal for the most part. "It made us stronger than we were before. I got closer to the children. I don't think the family has any emotional scars at all from my being out of work," said Steve, but added that he isn't over the pay cut.

"If I had a job that paid me what I was making before unemployment, I wouldn't feel anything about it. That still hasn't healed."

## COUPLES WITHOUT CHILDREN AT HOME

Gene and Teresa had lived with an empty nest for several years. In their early fifties, they were enjoying the good life on his computer programmer's salary for a leading Massachusetts high-tech firm. Then one fine New England fall day, his boss called him into his office and told him that the company was letting him go—the latest casualty in a "downsizing" of ten thousand employees.

It hurt, but the company helped. Gene picked up a hefty severance package based on his fifteen years' experience. He also signed on with the company's outplacement program and its career counselors. "The outplacement reinforced that they weren't cutting us loose because we weren't worthwhile, but because they were having a hard time. They told us that we were valuable, and that helped me accept the news."

Gene started his own interior design consulting service. He was able to pick up medical benefits through Teresa's part-time job at a child-care center. Teresa said, "We realize that we can live on a lot less than we thought. We can survive a while longer before we're hurting."

Although unemployment was hard, Gene and Teresa said the experience drew them together as a couple. Teresa helped Gene with his new business because she understood interior decorating. "When he worked in the computer business, I couldn't relate to it."

Gene's unemployment drew their children closer to them, too. Shortly before the layoff, he and Teresa set up a housing deal with their daughter and son-in-law. Gene and Teresa bought a condominium and sold their house at a loss to their daughter and son-in-law. When their daughter and son-in-law were later transferred, they sold the house at a profit, which paid off Gene's and Teresa's condo.

More important than the financial help from their daughter, however, unemployment opened the way for Gene and Teresa to grow closer to their estranged son. Gene used his time to do some carpentry work with his son. "This gave us a chance to get together and bond like we hadn't done for a while."

## SINGLE-PARENT FAMILIES

Unemployment is hard on virtually everyone. But no segment of the unemployed population has it as tough as single parents. They have all the hardships of singles and couples, with few of the advantages.

"With married couples, at least they've got a team. When you're single, it's just you," said Melinda, a divorced Texas mother of three school-age children. "When a bill doesn't get paid, the utilities get cut off. It's no wonder that women marry in this situation."

Melinda's divorce from her second husband—a wife abuser—had become effective a year earlier, and she was just recovering from being laid up for eight months with a broken back from an accident. She invested the rest of the accident settlement in a cosmetics franchise. She also worked at a private trade school, selling enrollments on a commission basis. But when her youngest son became sick, Melinda had to suspend her successful selling to care for him.

Her poverty devastated her mothering instinct. "I couldn't afford gifts. What hurt was that the church had to support me with food and Christmas presents. That hurt my pride terribly. I couldn't afford books for my son when he was in the hospital. There was a time when I didn't have any money, and I ate what he didn't eat on his plate."

Her first ex-husband played the children against her as well, she said. "If I grounded the kids or disciplined them, he would be more understanding and offer material things—things I couldn't give them."

At first, her children tried to comfort her with, "It's okay, Mom." But as the unemployment wore on, that attitude changed to, "*Dad* can give us these things."

Those pressures compounded the usual struggles of finding employment and maintaining her dignity. "If you don't have what society perceives as a good job," she said, "you have so many doubts. Even though you think there's something out there for you, it's horrible."

She listened to motivational cassette tapes, surrounded herself with encouraging friends, and knew when to stop pushing herself. If she worked hard, made half a dozen contacts in a day, and hit dry wells, she stopped. "I reached the point that I couldn't take another 'no' that day. I would tell myself, 'I did good today, and I will work on it tomorrow.' If I pushed too hard, the next day I wouldn't want to get out. I would drink. Then I wasn't motivated the next day."

Looking for work toughened her. "If someone rejected my idea, it wasn't a personal rejection. It was just that I was selling something that someone else didn't need. You cannot stay down in the pits; you've got to dig yourself out. The only way is to get out there."

Despite continued financial hardships, Melinda struggled and made it. She applied her sales skills to garner work for a court reporting firm. Her success at that job has attracted offers from other firms.

Melinda advises other single parents to remember, "The hard times of unemployment will pass; things will get better. You have to believe that, or you will not get a job. You will not be marketable. And to be marketable, you have to feel good about yourself."

But feeling good isn't found in yielding to the temptation of marrying for financial security, said Melinda, who has dated millionaires. It will backfire. "When things get bad between the two of you, then your husband refers to you as a freeloader. If you marry for a safety net, then you don't have a marriage."

Above all, Melinda recommends, don't get complacent—especially because single parents don't have the support systems of married couples. "The hardest thing was getting out of bed and putting on a business suit, even if I had nowhere to go. Then you look in the paper and network. It's very difficult some days. You want to stay at home, to hide inside those walls of your safe place."

TAKING CARE OF BUSINESS
To a greater or lesser extent, these families learned that they needed to trim their expenses and lifestyles. Oddly enough, people who should know better—namely, businessmen and businesswomen, or families whose breadwinners were executives—often practice denial by assuming that unemployment somehow isn't really affecting them. But if they conducted their businesses that way, they would drive their companies into the ground. At a time like this you may need to remind yourself, *tell the truth and cut the expenses.*

This is where you fine-tune the practice of telling the truth in love. How you present the needs for cutting back and for being resourceful may determine how much support you and your family members can give to each other. (Some of this information was discussed in chapter 5, but cutting expenses and the reasons behind it are worth closer examination here.)

Cut out what isn't essential: cable television, subscriptions to periodicals, and book and record clubs. Above all, delay major purchases: major appliances, a new car, or a vacation. If you've had a personal or family tradition of eating out on Sunday, for example, you'll need to let that tradition go in order to save money. Likewise, if you live in an expensive apartment and you have the opportunity to move into a cheaper place, take it. Learn to let go. Be flexible. Don't fall into the temptation to hang on to possessions or habits because you think they're the only things you have left during uncertain times.

The entire family needs to participate in this discussion, because your unemployment is a serious issue that affects everybody. Your decisions should not take anyone in the family by surprise. This communication is also a way to draw closer to your family in a very difficult time. Invite your children to make suggestions about what should you cut. Say to them, "Okay, kids. This is the income we believe we're going to have. This is what we need to cut back. If we don't cut back here, then where *do* we cut back?"

### Hidden Resources

Consider what you already have at home. In our materialistic culture, we tend to buy something new to replace something perfectly good that has simply gone out of fashion. It would be worthwhile for you to sort through your closets. You might find clothes you forgot about, or even pieces that are now back in fashion. If you can't use the clothing or other household items, sell them at a garage sale, give them to friends, or donate them to charity (and don't forget to ask for a receipt for tax time!).

Cleaning house or your apartment has other benefits as well. It clears the air by letting you and your family know that you are making a change in your life. It's also a good way to prepare yourself for a move. If you were to land a new job and had to move to a new city, what seems to have been an interminably long time of boredom and waiting will suddenly accelerate into chaos and panic. You can use the time now to clean—and save yourself time and trouble later.

### Food

The following tips can save you money and stretch your food dollars—long after your time of unemployment has ended.

*Grocery shopping.* Shopping for food and household supplies is one of the biggest ways you can cut back and learn resourcefulness. The techniques aren't new, but they take on new importance.

☞ Clip coupons. Look for stores that double their value.
☞ Eat before you go grocery shopping. When you shop on an empty stomach, you are more likely to yield to impulse buying.

☞ Make a list of what you need, and stick to that list.

☞ Buy generic food and household supplies, or look for the supermarket "house" brand.

☞ If you've tended to live high on the hog, shop for cheaper cuts of meat or less expensive ways to get your protein.

☞ Consult cookbooks for ways you can cook more cheaply, and then buy accordingly.

If you have a family, buy your food in larger quantities. If you are single, however, buying in large quantities may be an unwise decision, especially if the remaining food spoils or tempts you to overeat.

Remember that eating healthy costs no more, and may cost a lot less, than eating prepared or fast foods. This is not to say that treats are out of the question. You have to use your own judgment and balance other considerations when you shop. I don't believe that even when times are tough, you must cruise the aisles with a sour face, thinking, "I'll never be able to bake and eat brownies again."

As mentioned earlier, time is your greatest asset when you are unemployed. Learn to cook. It is a wonderful, creative release. You can do it whether you are married or single, with or without children. Ask your kids for their help in cooking and food preparation.

*Weight control programs can wait.* If you have been paying to stay on a structured weight control program, drop it. Many of these programs are expensive. The only exceptions are if you have a health problem and/or you are under a doctor's care. You need to cut back your food bill for more reasons than to fit into a size eight dress.

**Health Care**

Health insurance is critical. Steve and Barb were members of his company's Health Maintenance Organization, which cost $200 a month. After he lost his job, he made arrangements with his former employer to continue the HMO coverage through the provisions of the Consolidated Omnibus Budget Reconciliation Act of 1986 (COBRA), but their payments climbed to $450 a month. They kept the HMO through Barb's delivery of their fourth child, and then found a cheap short-term catastrophic health insurance policy. After that policy expired, they found a longer-term policy with the same firm. They always carried at least some policy, Steve said, because they knew if they had let it lapse they might not have been able to start a new one, especially if a family member had a potentially costly preexisting health condition.

But what do you do if you're out of work for more than eighteen months and your benefits under COBRA expire? You can shop for affordable coverage. Look for an insurance plan with a high deductible ($1,000 or $2,000), no wellness benefits, and/or no maternity coverage if you're sure you won't need it.

Also, explore health clinics—either government supported or through a university medical school—that offer basic medical care, child immunizations, and laboratory tests. Some community centers and churches offer low-cost or free medical clinics, too. Many have a sliding fee scale based on ability to pay.

### Recreation

These families found that they could enjoy recreation without having to pay small fortunes at theaters, restaurants, or ball parks. For example, Steve and Barb maintained their low-cost membership in their health club for family recreation and fitness. Because of their young children, they didn't eat out much. "We continued to rent movies, play putt-putt golf, and go swimming," they said. "We didn't try to make it a life-and-death situation every day." Grandparents helped by inviting the children to swim at their nearby beach.

If you belong to a health club, YMCA, or community organization, evaluate whether it's worth staying a member. If you don't benefit from it regularly, drop it. But if you and your family are actively using it, it may be worth keeping. Compared with other forms of entertainment, it can provide inexpensive recreation and a way for you to keep in shape. However, if your financial situation is desperate, close out the membership(s).

### CHARITY BEGINS AT HOME, BUT IT DOESN'T END THERE

People who have experienced unemployment will tell you that in such circumstances families will either drift apart or pull together—they rarely stay the same. You will find that you have resources you never imagined as you make your way through this time.

Sometimes, however, family means aren't enough to pay all the bills or keep food on the table. That's when you need to seek out the charities and other resources in your area that can help you. Knowing where to go and how to apply will save you money, time, headaches, and heartaches.

# CHAPTER ELEVEN

# Resourcefulness:
# Seeking Out Charity

J ames had studied hard, worked hard, and played hard. Then he lost his advertising job. For the first time in his life, he was faced with accepting food—without paying for it—from a community religious social service agency.

It was hard at first, but he found a church program where he could exchange his volunteer work at a soup kitchen for credits for food. "They had corn meal, flour, and tomatoes. You start rejoicing in the little things that come across. You learn that there are churches out there that will help you financially."

James found himself in a vulnerable position, and charity was one way to lessen his financial and emotional burdens. Like James, you will find that financial, personal, and family issues will radically affect your ability to provide for yourself and your family. Public and private social service agencies have a lot to offer when you're looking for food, utility payments, clothing, financial assistance, and counseling.

The earlier you seek help, the sooner your unemployment will be more tolerable. And you might even gain some valuable aid in your job search. But first, there's a matter of attitude you might need to consider.

## HELP, I NEED SOMEBODY

Receiving charity is the hardest part of being resourceful. Many of us are reluctant to accept charity, either because we were taught to be independent and self-reliant or because we think it's somehow "beneath" us.

To develop true resourcefulness, you need to let go of your pride. Pride will hinder you from seeking charity. And in the long run that could hurt you, your finances, your family, and your job search.

It used to be that "charity" was for low-income folks. Now with the changes in the economy—either the national economy or your own personal economy—you will find that "charity" is for all-income folks. It may feel strange to ask for and receive it. But unemployment is a strange time of life, and you need all the help you can find.

During your career, you have relied on your education or vocational training, your business sense, your common sense, and just plain hard work to support your family and yourself. Unemployment, however, means that you need to apply these and learn other skills to cope for the short-term. You may not know where to turn for assistance, and that can be frustrating. You may even think that nothing is available for you. Not true.

The secrets for finding charity are the same as looking for a job: knowing what you want, creativity, persistence, and networking. You need to know where to start and who to talk to.

The Rev. Carol Wylie directs the Ecumenical Social Ministries, a social service agency formed by a coalition of churches in Colorado Springs. She has had extensive experience dealing with private and public assistance programs and the people who use them. According to Carol, people make one of two errors as they approach their unemployment. "They either regard unemployment as a vacation, so they don't get involved with their own futures," she said. "On the other side, they are fearful and immobilized. Either way, the result is the same. They do nothing."

What follows are her suggestions to help you get started in dealing with charitable organizations.

GOVERNMENT ASSISTANCE

Help is available from a variety of federal, state, and local public assistance programs and departments. See the government pages in your phone book for the numbers and addresses of what or whom to contact.

**Federal**

The federal government, of course, is the biggest of bureaucracies. Consequently, help will take that much longer to obtain. These programs will be the most difficult to access. But they are worth looking into, especially if you are a senior citizen, are blind, or have children. Some of these programs are administered on a state or local level.

On the federal level, you may be able to receive assistance from these programs:

☞ Supplemental Security Income (SSI), a program for those who are physically impaired.

☞ Social Security Disabled Individual (SSDI).

☞ Food stamps (through the U.S. Department of Agriculture).

☞ The Job Training Partnership Act (JTPA), a program for lower-income people who need to retool their skills.

☞ Aid to Families with Dependent Children (AFDC).

☞ Senior Employment.

☞ Programs for the blind.

When you visit these or state or local agencies, be sure to bring your Social Security card, pay receipts from your former job, and names and addresses of former employers.

## State

State programs vary widely. They include workers' compensation and disabilities programs. Some states have programs in which you can donate time to charities, social service agencies, or soup kitchens. In turn, you can receive food or other assistance at low cost.

You've already been in touch with your state's unemployment insurance administration and Job Service. It's quite possible that people there may know where else you can turn, but keep in mind that they are not referral agencies or charitable organizations. However, Job Service probably will have a bulletin board with listings of jobs and places to find charity.

For further assistance, consult the government pages in your telephone book.

## Local

For connections to local public assistance programs, call your local Department of Social Services, library, or even police or fire departments. Regardless of what or who you call and the results you do or don't get, don't give up and don't feel ashamed. These agencies are in the business of helping people, and they aren't there to judge you. You have nothing to lose.

PRIVATE ASSISTANCE

The best, most accessible, and most helpful assistance will be on the private, local level.

There are a number of places you can start looking for help. The most convenient would be your place of worship. Most congregations either run their own programs or are in touch with local charitable organizations. They may even be able to help with cash payments for bills. Many congregations have food banks and even used clothing and furniture stores.

Don't hesitate to ask and don't be ashamed. People will probably find out anyway, so don't worry about it. If your friends think less of you for seeking help, you've got to wonder what kind of friends they are to begin with. I've known of people who have even disguised their appearance when going to their own church for help. You won't fool anyone.

Your congregation is only a start. If it doesn't have a program of charity, or you don't have a congregation to begin with, you have a number of resources as close as your phone book and telephone. Start your search by calling any one of a number of organizations: The United Way, United Appeal, the Red Cross, or the Salvation Army. Each of these organizations networks with others in your city, because they constantly provide referrals. Besides referrals, they need each other (for reasons that will be discussed later).

**First Impressions**

Whether it's romance, job hunting, or seeking charity, first impressions are very important. But the way you make a good first impression on a local charitable organization differs greatly from making a good first impression at an interview at a bank. You may not feel poor. But how you dress and behave yourself will matter a lot when you visit these organizations for the first time.

You can't help what kind of automobile you're driving. There are unemployed executives or middle managers who will feel strange driving to a social service agency in a luxury car. But don't flaunt it.

You can, however, do a great deal about your dress and personal grooming. Dressing too well will work against you when you visit a social service agency. Carol Wylie recommends that you dress decently, but don't wear a suit or your best dress. And don't wear jewelry. Otherwise, those working at the charity may wonder to themselves, "Is this guy's problem really so serious? Couldn't he just *sell* his gold watch?" Even though they know you can't eat your watch, they may be more hesitant to help you out. You want to appear common and blend in with the rest of the people.

## Humility
Maintain a humble attitude. Remember that you are one of hundreds or thousands of people with whom those on the other side of the counter at the social service agency must deal. You need to cooperate with them in order to let them know that you are serious about seeking assistance and pursuing the job hunt. The more you can let them know what you want and need without being pushy, the more they can help you.

However, don't let anybody—whether at a public or private agency— treat you poorly. You have the right to be treated with dignity and respect. How you respect yourself will go a long way in gaining the respect of others.

## Identify Yourself: Part One
The first thing that agency staff will ask you is, "Who are you, and can you prove it?" If you've been a decent, upstanding citizen all your life, you may very well resent this.

Regrettably, there are people who try to cheat or live off the system of charity that your community offers. They often do this by taking several names to collect as much as they can. But the reason that a charitable organization needs to know about you goes beyond their wariness of those who take advantage of the system.

These organizations are responsible to a wide variety of supporting individuals, corporations, religious congregations, and civic groups. You may have directly or indirectly supported them yourself. These supporters want to know, "Where does the money go? Is this charity using it responsibly?" Now that you're on the other end of it, you can see why they ask you for identification. This charity wants to get the best help for you, but you need to uphold some integrity standards yourself.

If you say you have a need, they will check it out. For example, if you tell them that you need bus fare to travel to a job interview in another city, they will call that employer and ask them if you really have a job interview. They aren't trying to humiliate you. They simply have scarce resources and are trying to help as many people as they can in the best and most efficient ways possible.

Showing identification has another purpose as well. Charitable organizations already have associations with similar groups, often on computer networks. When you give them your identification and outline your needs, they can log that information on their computer to let the other charities know what you and your family need, as well as monitor your job search.

Many agencies have added a job component to the other services and goods they offer. They ask what skills you have and what types of work—whether part-time, temporary, or permanent—you would be able to take. Whether they ask you or not, you should be willing to volunteer your services at the agency. You may be able to barter your time there for other goods and services from that agency or others in the community.

When you go to the local charity, bring a Social Security card, a driver's license with your picture on it, or some other form of legal identification. Also, bring some form of proof of your employment history and a list of marketable skills. But you don't need as much identification as you did when you filed for unemployment insurance benefits.

### Identify Yourself: Part Two
Bring more than your identification, however. Before you go, think through your short- and long-range goals. You don't need a detailed outline. Also, take an inventory of your assets, liabilities, income, and bills. Remember that you need to think clearly and deal with the future even more than you need bread or short-term cash. *Be honest*. People at the agency will be much more willing and able to help you if you know your budget and what you want. They can make the best referrals when they know your financial situation. You've got some momentum when you can identify your assets and goals.

Do not bring a list of demands. Don't walk into a charitable organization and ask, "What have you got?" as though you are shopping at a supermarket where you can pick up one of this and two of that.

Having said that, though, going to a social service agency early in your unemployment will give you a better idea of what may be available to you—and save you headaches months down the road. Many employees and volunteers at charities know how to help you plan, budget your money, and guide you in refining your goals. They may also be able to advise you with some tips for use at a later date. For example, if you've had a good credit record with your utility companies, the agency may be able to write a letter of reference for you if you later are so financially strapped that you need to delay paying a bill for a month.

If you wait to register with an agency until right before you are about to have your home foreclosed or your lights shut off, it can't do as much for you. In rare instances, you may be able to coax a cash payment from it. But you, the agency, and your creditors would have been better off had you signed up earlier.

These social service agencies are usually well connected to the business community and may be able to help with your networking. Additionally, they often carry job listings for part-time or temporary employment.

OTHER RESOURCES

The public, private, and religious charities and social service agencies aren't the only resources available. The following resources will also help you help yourself as you make your way through unemployment:

**Libraries**

Your local public library is one of the best—and cheapest—resources imaginable. It will provide:

☞ Federal and state publications on careers, jobs, and economic trends.

☞ Newspapers from your town and major cities. The papers list classified ads for jobs and temporary help.

☞ Telephone books (now usually on microforms) from every major city in the country.

☞ Periodicals related specifically to your trade and profession.

☞ Reference books for accessing newspapers and periodicals.

☞ Possible job listing boards.

Ask the reference librarians for help. They have had experience in guiding unemployed persons in their searches for charity and jobs. And of course, they carry thousands of books, videos, sound recordings, and other materials. These are important for your own self-education. Learn something. Don't just park yourself in front of the television after a discouraging day of phone calls and job hunting.

### Local Colleges and Universities
Institutions of higher learning also may be able to offer you resources for surviving unemployment. They have libraries, although your ability to check out materials may be restricted if you aren't a student. But you will be able to browse the books. They will also have more journals specifically related to your field of work.

Colleges and universities also offer speakers, films, and other forms of education and entertainment that are cheaper than most commercial amusements.

### Community Centers
Local community centers offer classes—sometimes very good vocational training classes. They have organized athletics, speakers, and family programs. And they provide a place for you to network, either socially or through job listing boards.

Both colleges and community centers offer self-help programs, too. One single mom has benefited from a course for women to bolster their self-esteem. "They talk about what you have to contribute," she says. "It helps to redefine your thinking, instead of letting society define who you are. They give recommendations for how to dress, how to wear your hair—and to smile even when you don't feel like it."

### The YMCA
The YMCA and similar religiously founded community organizations still carry some of the best athletic and family programs around. They, too, offer great opportunities for you to network as you sweat it out in aerobics classes or the weight room.

### YOU CAN'T EAT STATUS
Unemployment will teach you more lessons than you ever wanted to learn. One of them is that issues of social status—often based on your money and income—are very fleeting. Investing loyalty in status is too high a risk. You may find out that such status won't help you much now. So be resourceful and seek help.

Realize that your pride isn't worth hanging on to. There's no shame in going for help, even if you feel there is. Do not wait to seek charity.

Whatever you do, *don't give up*. Just because several agencies told you they can't help you or can do only a little doesn't mean you should quit trying. Be creative in your thinking and searching. You *will* find help, and the sooner you do so the stronger you will be in the long run. The personal strength you build up in the process will enable you to resist temptations and employment scams that tear at your soul or gouge you in the wallet.

# CHAPTER TWELVE

# Guard Your Soul: Temptations

I f you are unemployed, you are vulnerable to temptation. Your vulnerability is a consequence of what you have lost and what you don't have. These losses include a steady source of income, financial security, status, and possibly marital and family stability. You may be reeling from depression, stress, indirection, and strained friendships as well. You may feel numb, discouraged, lonely, and powerless.

Regardless of your moral fiber or how strong your support systems may be, you should be aware that your resistance to temptation is probably apt to be low. This isn't intended to scare you, but to help you in a matter-of-fact way to recognize that vices you would never have given a second thought to could now cause you immense harm if you succumb to them.

I CAN RESIST ANYTHING EXCEPT TEMPTATION

It's 8:00 p.m. You've made two dozen phone calls and knocked on doors all day. You're wrapping up another hour of job research at the local library and face going home to a tense family situation. The kids are too loud and the spouse nags you too much. The bills are piling up as the savings account is going down. So you head for the local tavern where you can commiserate with your buddies—including buddies of the opposite sex—who've also lost their jobs. One thing leads to another.

It's an old story. The reasons for affairs, and for indulging in a variety of other temptations and vices, are understandable. And the results of giving in are as destructive as ever.

These sins didn't get their reputation because they felt bad—at least not at first. Affairs, substance abuse, binge spending, and gambling are symptoms of deeper issues. They all ride on the desire to get a thrill from something. You feel dead, you feel worthless. So something comes along that will affirm you, make you feel good, or give you a rush to escape the pain. On the other hand, the sins of family violence feel bad for everyone from start to finish. Yet they, too, have their roots in a desire to solve a problem right away.

Although the going up is not worth the coming down—with its apologies, remorse, and promises to do better—these cycles of abusive behavior tend to escalate. This is basic addictive behavior, and it afflicts millions of people. Whether or not you are drawn into this behavior during normal times, you need to know that the desires will intensify when you are unemployed.

History proves that human nature knows no limits on destructive behavior, from sexual lust to world wars. What follows are brief summaries of five temptations that pose the greatest threats to you and your family's stability during unemployment. Knowing that you're vulnerable to them and their consequences can arm you with the strength to resist them when they come along.

AFFAIRS

If you are married, you've probably invested years in forging a deep relationship. Unemployment will test that relationship in the ways you use your time, budget your money, and hope for the future. An hour of pleasure in an affair will throw it all on the rocks for years to come, if not for the rest of your life.

**Consider the Consequences**

An affair will have terrible consequences. Consider any or all of these results when you are tempted:

- ☞ Compounded shame on top of your job loss.
- ☞ Additional and crushing stress on your marriage.
- ☞ Separation or divorce.
- ☞ Alimony payments.
- ☞ Child-support payments.
- ☞ Sexually transmitted diseases.

☞ Wrecked career plans.

☞ The indescribable pain of all of the above.

## Head Off Opportunities for an Affair Before It Begins

Knowing the scenarios for an affair may help you resist the temptation, too. Here are several basic settings that could set you up for an affair:

*Bonding with others who have been laid off or fired.* You will naturally share pain and sympathy for those who have lost their jobs. If your spouse is not supportive, or if you simply *perceive* that your spouse is not supportive, you are more likely to gravitate toward someone who knows what you are going through. The intimacy of sharing about this deep and traumatic experience will accelerate the sexual dynamic.

*Bonding with coworkers who have been laid off or fired.* The same elements as above are at work here, but the dynamics are even stronger. You may have spent more waking hours with coworkers than living with your spouse or other family members. You have both seen up close the other's pain—as well as the attraction.

*Excessive attachment to your job.* Being "married to your job" is more than a cute cliché about your attachment to your work. You may have invested love, time, energy, money, drive, and desire in your work in a way that mimics the marriage vows of "for better for worse, for richer for poorer, in sickness and in health." When job loss severs that "working relationship," you may grieve as if you had lost your spouse—and you may want to find a new relationship. But if work isn't available, and your work had become your "first love," you may not know how to relate to your spouse. You might then seek reassurance from someone of the opposite sex.

*Time on your hands.* If both you and your spouse work, and you lose your job, you may have a lot of time on your hands. Discouragement in the job hunt coupled with time to drown your sorrows may leave you especially vulnerable to the temptation of an affair.

*A power vacuum.* If you had a job in which you held power, and you've lost that power, you may want to regain at least the shadow of it through an affair.

Your situation may not fit any of these possibilities, but you need to be aware of them and guard yourself through communication with your spouse, counseling with a trusted professional or member of the clergy, and prayer. For the sake of your family, your finances, and your future, *do not ignore the warning signs of an affair.*

If you're single, you don't have a marriage to lose, but you don't have its support, either. You're then tempted by the desire to seek comfort in the arms of as many people as possible. You won't have immediate family members to damage with this kind of promiscuity, but you will damage your own soul in the process.

FAMILY VIOLENCE

The temptation to commit acts of violence against family members—whether against a spouse, children, or parents—may increase as a result of unemployment. For example, the National Committee for Prevention of Child Abuse reported that deaths from child abuse increased 10 percent in the early 1990s, and commented that the increase reflected the hard economic times of the recession that began in 1990.

You resent it that you have time on your hands. You resent it when your children cry and make demands on you. You resent it that even your family's basic needs for food, clothing, shelter, and transportation chip away at your scarce resources. You resent taking charity to fill in the gaps. The problems compound, such as delaying treatment for a spouse's or a child's illness. The erosion of your resources puts that much more pressure on your job search.

If you don't channel that irritation and anger in a healthy direction, domestic violence or child abuse may result. If your marriage and/or family life has been strained and you were highly attached to your job, unemployment will confront you with the temptation to strike out. Substance abuse, an affair, or gambling will exacerbate the stresses that lead to domestic violence.

This is especially true if you have had a "macho" job with heavy physical demands, or even a high-powered management position. These jobs rely on muscle and ego. That's how things got done. Husbands, especially, will feel impotent having lost their jobs, but they can feel powerful again by lashing out physically against weaker family members.

Relieving your frustrations violently will cause great damage. The long-term effects will devastate your family relationships and undermine your ability to get along with people in general, especially when you are looking for new employment.

**Guarding Against Committing Family Violence**

You can take several steps to check the urge to abuse those you love and those who love you.

First, *keep communication lines open*. Let your spouse and children know that unemployment is tough, and that you might be tempted to react in inappropriate ways. This is not an excuse, but an invitation for them to let you know when you are getting hot under the collar and remind you to please calm down.

Second, home life will proceed that much more smoothly, and the awkward time of unemployment will end faster, if you can look for a job undisturbed. If you have children at home, especially if you had to pull them out of day care, make it clear to them that you aren't to be disturbed while you're job hunting, doing research, or talking on the telephone.

Third, when you get the urge to hit or be verbally abusive, take these steps recommended by Thomas Gordon and the National Committee for Prevention of Child Abuse:

1. Take a deep breath. And another. Then remember *you* are the adult.
2. Close your eyes and imagine you're hearing what your child is about to hear.
3. Press your lips together and count to ten. Or better yet, to twenty.
4. Put your child in a time-out chair. (Remember this rule: One timeout minute for each year of age.)
5. Phone a friend.
6. If someone else can watch the children, go outside and take a walk.
7. Take a hot bath or splash cool water on your face.
8. Hug a pillow.
9. Turn on some music. Maybe even sing along.
10. Pick up a pencil and write down as many helpful words as you can. Save the list.

When the urge to strike passes, hug them and let them know that you love them. But if the urge doesn't pass—or the problem of family violence is heading out of control—seek professional help immediately. Contact your clergyman, your local mental health association, your local Family Service America organization, or your community or county department of social services.

If you or your children are victims of violence, *get out of the house*.

No case of unemployment, or its resulting anguish, should be accepted as an excuse for a spouse or parent hitting or otherwise abusing family members. Your community probably has a shelter for battered spouses and/or children. Contact your community's department of social services or mental health association for its location.

SUBSTANCE ABUSE

When you're unemployed, the job search is going nowhere, your future looks bleak, and you feel intense stress, you want to feel *something,* good or bad. Maybe you want to feel nothing. You want to alter your mood by speeding up, slowing down, or dropping out. A host of substances will do that for you—at least for a time.

People who can barely find the cash to pay the rent or utilities always seem able to scrape enough together to buy tobacco, alcohol, illegal drugs, or junk food. Financial advisors and investors, in fact, can count on stocks in alcohol and tobacco companies to rise during recessions.

But the problem of trying to drown your sorrows is that your sorrows always find a way of floating to the surface. The risks of substance abuse have been widely publicized, but they most pointedly affect the unemployed person in several ways. Mood-altering substances cost an immense amount, and they cost you the most when you can afford them the least. They take money away from those bills you and your family need to pay for your own survival. Many are, of course, habit-forming. And once those habits are in place, they take a long time to dislodge, even after you are able to find employment again. Then they interfere with your future employment either through the immediate consequences of the substances themselves, impaired mental stability, or lowered resistance to disease.

Most warnings about substance abuse are directed at tobacco, alcohol, cocaine, marijuana, and other drugs. But food, too, is a substance that can be abused. People who would never think of smoking a joint or guzzling a six-pack of beer will binge on food. Aside from the immediate effects of altering your moods by making you feel uncomfortably bloated, overeating will cause weight gain (another blow to your self-esteem) and other health problems.

BINGE SPENDING

One of the oddest temptations that newly unemployed people face is the urge to spend money—sometimes a lot of money. People will inexplicably take expensive vacations, embark on shopping sprees, or redecorate their homes. If they don't have the cash, they will max out their credit cards. These irrational acts serve no purpose other than to mask the pain of joblessness.

For many people, shopping is a mood-altering act, just like abusing substances. We live in a consumer-oriented, materialistic society. We are exposed to a constant barrage of advertisements trying to convince us that buying products will make us happy.

Things can make you happy, but not for long. The consequences of binge spending will return to haunt you far more quickly when you're unemployed than when you have a job.

Before you invade the mall, brandishing your credit card, remember these things:

☞ Regardless of the "available balance" on your credit limit, remember that *you can't afford to do this*.

☞ You will damage your precious credit rating.

☞ Every dollar you spend on something frivolous is a dollar less you will have to spend on the necessities of survival.

☞ Many credit cards charge as much as 20 percent interest. So the $1,000 you blow on a shopping spree could cost you as much as $200 in interest in a year's time.

☞ Think of your family members who will suffer because you do this. If you're single, think about what this will do to your ability to survive unemployment.

GAMBLING

Binge spending can't hold a lottery ticket to the temptation of gambling as a way to gain some fast wealth or mask pain. Gambling has skyrocketed in recent years because of the availability of race tracks, off-track betting, bingo games, and casinos in many cities and on Indian reservations. More than any other influence, though, the availability of lotteries in more than thirty states makes it very tempting to take the few dollars you receive in change at the gas station or the convenience store and spend it on lottery tickets.

Gambling incorporates three elements: (1) the risk of a smaller investment to gain a far larger payoff; (2) an artificial means of chance: either an event that is hard to predict, such as a sporting contest, or an event with an unpredictable outcome, such as the draw of a card or the yank on the lever of a slot machine; (3) the losses of the many support the winnings of the few.

In other words, when you gamble *you lose*. A few people do know how to work the odds against the casino or the track. Some say they even know how to work the odds of a lottery. But that's the few. The majority of people who gamble do it for the thrill and the foolish notion that wealth can be created without work. You're paying someone for the chance to take money from someone else. Gambling doesn't produce anything, except for those who run the gambling industry.

Valerie Lorenz, director of the Compulsive Gambling Center in Baltimore, said that although hard statistical evidence isn't available yet, she and other analysts have found more than a casual correlation between unemployment and gambling. For example, they've found that people who retire have less income as well as more time on their hands. So they go to a casino or track to fill up the time with the hope that they can bolster their income.

On a more sinister note, Valerie said that Maryland had few if any beatings in the past twenty years as a result of gamblers' failures to pay their bookies. But as the economy went sour with the recession that began in 1990, the incidence of gambling went up, and so did the beatings.

For the unemployed who are tempted to gamble, there are several serious ramifications:

1. The money adds up. A few bucks on lottery tickets here, a few bucks on bingo there—that's money that isn't going to bills, food, rent, mortgage, or insurance.

2. You buy into the delusion that gambling will solve your financial problems. They won't, because the odds are against you. Odds on winning the "scratch" games vary from state to state, according to Valerie Lorenz. But statistically, you have a much greater chance of being struck by lightning than winning the jackpot of a state lottery.

3. You risk becoming addicted to gambling, Valerie said. As with drug abuse, there is a certain percentage of people (between 3 percent to 7 percent of the general public) who will turn into compulsive gamblers. The rate of addiction is higher among teenagers. The results—besides the money you fritter away—include deceit and theft to support the habit and the downward spiral of thrill, depression, family violence, and possibly even suicide.

These are risks and habits you will carry with you beyond the time of your unemployment. Even if you win—and *no* gambling activity is weighed in favor of the player—you still face the working world.

If you are tempted to buy a lottery ticket or play the slots, *think hard* about what that money could buy. Even a few dollars spent on a lottery ticket could buy your children a treat or pay the interest on an outstanding bill.

If you have yielded to the temptation to gamble, contact the Compulsive Gambling Center, 924 E. Baltimore St., Baltimore, MD 21202, or call their hot-line at 1-800-332-0402. You can also check your phone book for the local chapter of Gamblers Anonymous.

GETTING HELP
Gamblers Anonymous is one of a variety of twelve-step programs for those who are addicted. Others include the well-known Alcoholics Anonymous, as well as groups for those with dependencies on money or sex and those who are spouse- and child-abusers.

If you or an unemployed loved one struggles with these or other temptations that hurt your finances, family, and future, get help by calling these organizations. Also contact your minister, priest, or community mental health center. The sooner you can break the grip of these temptations, the better able you will be to focus on surviving unemployment and finding new work.

When your self-esteem is in place and something happy comes along, you experience a genuine, life-affirming joy and happiness. But the thrills of these dangerous temptations don't affirm life. Some are downright destructive. They are not worth the pain they cause.

Unfortunately, moral temptations are not the only areas in which you need to stay on guard. You also need to watch your back for those who are out to scam the unemployed.

# CHAPTER THIRTEEN

# Watch Your Back: Employment Scams

❖

F rank had diligently searched for new employment since he lost his $110,000-per-year management position five months earlier. Then he noticed an ad in a leading business periodical for an executive with extensive high-tech and international experience. He promptly sent off a response.

Three weeks later, he received a large envelope with a return address from New York City's business district. The cover letter on top of a stack of forms glowed with compliments for Frank: "You have the qualifications we've been looking for as we lead our company into the next decade of growth. Please review and complete the attached forms so we may process your application and set up an interview."

Frank grew more excited about this dream corporation as he thumbed through the forms, until he came to the last page. "Please return the completed documents along with a $5,000 processing fee to this address. . . ."

Frank was lucky. He caught on to the scam before the scam could catch him.

WHAT'S THE SCAM, SAM?
Unfortunately, the sins of the flesh discussed in chapter 12 aren't the only temptations you may face during your unemployment. There are people out there who are more than happy to take advantage of your vulnerability, as well as your money, by snaring you in one of a variety of scams that prey on the unemployed. If you fall victim to such a scam,

you will lose money as well as self-esteem. The only thing you will gain is even more discouragement in your job hunt.

Vicky Barber, an investigator for the consumer fraud division of the Colorado Attorney General's office, says that these scams increase during times of war, reconstruction, and recession: "When times are tough, these things pop up all over the place."

Garth Lucero, the lead attorney in the consumer fraud division, adds that people are vulnerable when they are unemployed, and so they're ripe for being taken: "You've got a captive audience."

Don't think you aren't vulnerable. Vicky and Garth say that the potential victims don't fit a standard profile. They've seen unskilled laborers as well as doctors and lawyers fall for any one of a variety of schemes, from fee-based executive searches to bait-and-switch help wanted ads.

"What bothers me," Vicky said, "is high school kids who see ads for fork lift drivers for nine dollars an hour. The kids show up at the agency, whose representatives tell the kids that the fork lift jobs have been filled. But the representatives have jobs for the kids at five dollars an hour working on a dock."

Imagination has no limits in devising schemes to fleece the innocent. There are, however, several types of scams that have endured over the years. Watch for these as you conduct your job search. Being cautious will not only save your dignity, but you may save thousands of dollars as well. And remember the first rule of scam vigilance: "If it sounds too good to be true, it is."

## EDUCATION SCAMS
An education is a wonderful thing—except when students borrow thousands of dollars to spend on bogus trade schools set up by unscrupulous people. These schools advertise for courses in legitimate trades such as cosmetology, truck driving, cooking, or hair design. But they engage in a variety of deceptive practices:

    ☞ They often recruit students by passing out literature at unemployment offices.
    ☞ They promise thorough training, often in a short period of time.
    ☞ They claim an amazing graduation rate.
    ☞ They guarantee employment.

☞ They promise students that they will learn enough to be licensed by the appropriate state certification board or agency.

☞ They tell students they have inside connections to businesses.

☞ They arrange student loans, but they don't tell students about refund policies.

This last deception has caused the most heartache for unsuspecting students. These fraudulent vocational schools will encourage prospective students to register, regardless of the students' aptitude for a trade or academics. They arrange student loans, regardless of the students' ability to pay. Then when this kind of school enrolls enough students, it files for bankruptcy. Vicky and Garth say it may be difficult to prove unlawful conduct on the part of the school unless the school officials engage in blatantly inappropriate activities—such as taking students' tuition when they know the school is financially insolvent and will soon close its doors.

The students are then stuck without an education, without a trade, without a job—and with a loan of several thousand dollars. Regardless of what happens to the vocational school's managers, the students still have to repay those loans.

You can protect yourself from such frauds, said Garth Lucero. The state agency or board that licenses business, vocational, and occupational schools can tell you if the board has received complaints against the school. You may want to call local businesses in the school's trade—trucking firms, for example—for references. Also, check your local Better Business Bureau. Most trade schools are legitimate, but you owe it to yourself to research the circumstances prior to investing your scarce unemployment dollars.

JOB INFORMATION AND EMPLOYMENT AGENCY SCAMS

"Airlines Hiring Now!" "Careers Overseas!" "Australia Wants You!" Wow! And all you have to do is call—and then pay a fee.

Most companies that place help wanted ads are on the level. Even job information companies are legitimate—if they are up front with you and tell you that they charge a fee for the information they provide, usually consolidated from various sources.

But you should be skeptical of those few job agencies that claim to have an inside track in a specific industry. These companies falsely represent their alleged affiliations or connections with other companies. They may falsely represent the benefits of their goods and services. They may make guarantees of employment without explicitly stating what those guarantees are. They won't disclose details about what they promise. And after they've suckered you with their sales pitch and you agree to accept their services, they ask for up-front fees—sometimes an exorbitant amount for what you get.

For example, let's say an employment agency claims it can put you in touch with jobs in the airline industry: flight attendants, mechanics, even pilots. You call and they say they have information not available to the public. You may go to their office where they spell out what they can do for you. You may sign up with them, and then they charge you.

Sometimes these agencies simply advertise for "job listings." These scams are simple. You mail them $14.95—or $29.95, or more—and get an envelope with newspaper clippings of classified ads or booklets with airlines' names and addresses and descriptions of airline-related jobs.

What's so sad about this is that you can get the same information for free by directly contacting the companies. For example, you can just call the airline's personnel office about available jobs.

These bogus employment agencies—sometimes taking names that sound similar to legitimate corporations—also engage in high-pressure tactics. Beware if an agency representative says, "We have a connection to Big Bux, Inc. But you could lose the opportunity to work for them if we don't get your processing fee by five p.m. today."

Also be wary of employment agencies or their representatives who do any of these:

☞ Offer guaranteed employment.
☞ Ask for full, non-refundable payment in advance, without any provision for paying on an increment basis.
☞ Dazzle you with a bogus phone conversation. For example, you're sitting in their office, the phone rings, and the representative answers, saying, "He got the job? At fifty thousand a year? Great!" And then he puts down the phone, turns to you with a smile, and says, "We helped him last week."
☞ Will take money only in certified funds: cash, cashier's checks, or money orders. (They won't take personal checks

because they can be stopped.) And then they ask for it by over-night mail.

☞ Ask to meet you in a motel room (by the airport!).

Vicky and Garth have encountered other fly-by-night businesses that advertise a large number of jobs—such as bodyguards—for "immediate placement." These businesses will make urgent statements such as, "We need to place nine hundred bodyguards right away." They rent out a warehouse or meeting room in a hotel. Hundreds of people show up and fill out applications. Representatives from the business then say to each would-be bodyguard, "Everything looks fine. Now we just need seventy-five dollars from you to conduct a background check for security reasons." The representatives take the money and drive to the next state. The jobs never existed.

Often these unscrupulous employment agencies or job information companies will do business in your state, but not in the state in which the companies' offices are located. For example, some job information companies appeal to Persian Gulf War veterans who want to cash in on rebuilding Kuwait. They often have fancy, upscale addresses. They take out ads in other states. When people respond, the company sends them forms to fill out and charges "processing" fees, from several hundred to several thousand dollars. But the jobs, the applicants find out too late, didn't exist. And because the company's offices are in another state, the applicants are unable to get their money back.

CAREER COUNSELING SCAMS

A legitimate, professional career counselor can greatly assist you in focusing on what you want to do, writing résumés, and prepping for interviews. They offer hands-on assistance and how-to suggestions so you can be more effective in your job hunt.

But legitimate career counselors are shadowed by scam artists. These bogus career counselors may offer similar help, but they promise a lot more. Garth Lucero says their biggest claim is access to a "hidden" job market. They gain your confidence when they tell you they have inside information and they can do your networking for you.

Of course, this information isn't cheap. They often will ask you for your salary range and charge a percentage of that. So if you tell them you're looking for a $50,000-a-year position, they will ask for some percentage of that figure. However, the information they give you is hardly different than the information they would give to someone seeking a salary of half that.

They promise inside information that you could have found on your own (assuming it exists to begin with) and raise your expectations. But when the dream job doesn't materialize, they fall back on the defense that they were only going to provide the how-to.

Legitimate career counselors don't do this. They charge by the hour. And when you seek help from them, and then want to discontinue the service, the help ends there. They don't make promises of employment or brag about inside information. Also, they don't demand a non-refundable fee up front.

BUSINESS SCAMS

"Work at home! Low hours, high pay! Be your own boss!"

Business scams are among the most notorious and costly schemes that prey on the unemployed, especially those who are hard-working and have considered self-employment. They include:

- ☞ "Business opportunities" such as vending machines, finance programs, and real estate.
- ☞ Franchises for upstart businesses. "If you can pull together five or ten thousand dollars, we can set you up."
- ☞ Distributorships and pyramid schemes in which you work from your home. You buy thousands of dollars of products, recruit others to buy from you, who recruit others to buy from them, and so on.
- ☞ Investment scams in which you are encouraged to sink money into unknown banks or companies in order to reap a profit.

Many franchises are legitimate. However, the unemployed person may not be able to readily discern the differences between legitimate businesses and scams. The scams can be as small as selling modern snake oil or as big as drilling for real oil. The promoters inflate income projections and success stories, exploiting people with an entrepreneurial spirit.

These business scams damage your self-esteem when you realize that you've been taken. But even worse, they can fleece you for far more than the other scams listed above. They may also draw you into their own legal snare, so if they are taken to court you may have to go down with them. You owe it to yourself to think long and hard and count the cost before you decide to go into business for yourself. Make sure the business is one you can handle, and make the choice yourself. Be especially wary of people pushing the kinds of businesses I just listed.

## DIAL 1-900-RIPOFF

Although many scams have been around for years, they've recently gotten a technological boost from the advent of 900 telephone numbers. These pay-per-call services sell everything from sex to conversations with rock stars. And now they sell bogus job information.

Some of the companies behind 900 numbers (or local 976 and long-distance 700 exchanges) are legitimate. They tell you the cost of the whole call or the rate per minute. They also tell you what sort of information you will be hearing, such as the names and addresses of prospective companies. Some of it might be good consolidated information from a number of sources.

But the illegitimate job telemarketers can rip you off in a number of ways. First, they don't tell you how much the call will cost. Once you call—and you have to listen to the very end to get all the information—you may discover that the job was taken. Sometimes the recorded message or operator might speak so fast that you must call the number several times in order to write down all the information. The information you may hear could have been found for free by reading the want ads in the newspaper. And of course, you really pay when you get your phone bill.

Garth Lucero says that some people have caught on to the 900 number fraud and won't call them anymore. So the ever-cagey telemarketers have come up with a new twist on the scam. They advertise that you can find job information by calling a toll-free 800 number. You call and hear a recorded message telling you, "For more information, call 1-900. . . ."

If you have been caught in such a scam, the Federal Trade Commission suggests that you ask the phone company to delete the charge, although it's not legally obligated to do so.

You also can find out the company name and address of the 900 number from the phone company, then write the 900 number company and ask it to delete the charge. The company can refuse, and have a debt-collection agency contact you. You can then contact the debt collection agency and tell it not to contact you. Under the law, once the collection agency receives your letter, it cannot contact you again except to say there will be no further contact or that some specific action will be taken. You also may want the incident recorded on your credit report.

## SO WHAT DO YOU DO?

If you think you are being victimized, you can notify a variety of consumer and law enforcement agencies from the local to the federal level. Locally, contact the Better Business Bureau or the district attorney's office. On the state level, contact the attorney general's office and/or any agency that regulates the type of business or product. For example, if you've been victimized or think you'll be victimized by a fly-by-night trade school, contact the state agency that licenses trade schools.

You have numerous options on the federal level, too. The Federal Trade Commission is the most obvious, but there are others. If a fraudulent business is pushing an employment scam through the mail, contact the postal inspector. If it's by phone, that's wire fraud and would be investigated by the Federal Bureau of Investigation.

These overworked agencies will probably not jump on your complaint. They can't serve as your personal attorney. Sometimes a consumer agency will have to get a number of complaints before they take action. But every complaint throws a match on the woodpile. Your complaint may be the one that ignites an investigation.

Laws on employment scams vary from state to state. Usually, this sort of fraud is considered a violation of consumer protection laws—a misdemeanor, not a felony. These cases are often hard to pursue because the scam artists work across state lines, knowing that the states probably won't pursue them. But that doesn't mean you should give up.

Garth Lucero says that some of these shady outfits will respond if an attorney general's office contacts them and tells them that a citizen has registered a complaint. These outfits will deny that they've done anything wrong, but will make restitution to keep their names clear. The more people complain, the more likely these outfits are to clean up their act.

Even if you don't get your money back, it still may be therapeutic for you to file an official complaint. It can't hurt to let law enforcement agencies know about a possible ripoff operation. At least you'll have the satisfaction that you've done something, and satisfaction is a precious feeling during unemployment.

## JOB HUNTER BEWARE!

To protect yourself from scams of all types, there are several things you should *never* do, especially when you are dealing with prospective employers, job information agencies, or companies that want to set you up in business. *When talking to a stranger on the phone, never divulge:*

- ☞ Your Social Security number.
- ☞ Your driver's license number.
- ☞ Your credit card numbers.
- ☞ Your checking account numbers.
- ☞ Your savings account numbers.
- ☞ Details of your employment and salary history.
- ☞ Details of your personal finances and investments.

These and other personal details are just that—*personal*. If someone persists, ask for his or her name, the name of the company, phone number, street address, and state of incorporation. If they aren't willing to give you this basic information—which is public record for any business—hang up. If the calls continue, contact the telephone company and file a complaint.

## SAD BUT TRUE

The saddest part about scams that prey on the unemployed is that those who set them up know they are trying to take advantage of vulnerable people. Except in rare cases when you report them and the state or federal government takes action, there is little you can do to stop them. But if you're armed with the proper information, you can at least protect yourself, your time, and your cash—and spend your energy on seeking legitimate employment.

# CHAPTER FOURTEEN

# Part-Time Work, Temporary Work, Self-Employment

———————◆◆———————

H ugh's high-flying career as an engineer crashed one day, along with those of several hundred other employees, when his firm eliminated his department overnight. After the shock wore off, Hugh spent several months looking for a firm that was interested in his skills. Nothing panned out, so he decided to strike out on his own.

He had always wanted to try his hand at starting and running his own business. Hugh had the drive and the entrepreneurial spirit. He also had capital in the form of a hefty severance package—with pay and benefits at the level of when the company let him go—that would last eight months. And he had an idea he borrowed from something he remembered from his former company—running a mobile dry-cleaning service. "The engineering firm had a dry cleaner on site. You could drop your clothes off at work," he said. At the end of the working day, the employees could pick up their dry cleaning without the hassles of taking time off from work to drive to a laundry.

Hugh eyed several options. He quickly ruled out working for several months with an existing dry-cleaning company. He contemplated buying into one of several mobile dry-cleaning service franchises, costing from $15,000 to $20,000. Or he could go into business for himself.

He chose the last option and plowed much of his severance into the business. Compared with investing in a franchise, Hugh's new mobile dry-cleaning service had low start-up and maintenance costs. Profit margins were thin, but he could live with that initially.

Hugh liked dealing with people. He loved the independence. But the sixty-hour weeks grew old after half a year. Hugh said, "I'm going through the withdrawal now. At first, I was going to be the entrepreneur. But lately, I started looking at myself. As I get closer to that last severance check, reality is going to set in. I don't know if it's second thoughts or cold feet."

## WATCH YOUR BACK, PART TWO

Hugh isn't alone in his experiences. A significant percentage of the work force is self-employed or in part-time and temporary positions. Temporary work, in particular, is the employment wave of the future. But just because it's the wave of the future doesn't mean that it will happily wash up on your beach. You need to know some of the opportunities and some of the pitfalls of taking on such work.

For most unemployed persons, however, part-time or temporary work is necessary to stay afloat financially before getting into a new full-time job or career, or you may be able to farm out your skills and become self-employed. Temporary agencies can help. These agencies provide opportunities to help you hone old talents or learn new skills. Above all, a part-time or temporary job can show prospective permanent employers that you didn't take unemployment lying down, and that you were willing to learn new skills as well.

But you need to take some precautions. Be wary of sweatshops or companies that exploit their workers. Watch out for the employment scams discussed in chapter 13. And know your rights as an employee.

The most important precaution, however, concerns your own future. Regrettably, many talented, educated, and motivated workers get caught in a trap of seeking part-time or temporary work, hop from job to job, and forget their long-term needs and goals. Your primary goal is to find a new permanent job. A cycle of low-paying, part-time jobs will distract you from this objective, discourage you in your job search, and diminish your self-esteem. But if you keep your wits about you and stay focused on your future, part-time and temporary work can be a financial godsend. It might even open career doors to you that you never imagined.

## PART-TIME WORK

If after cutting back on expenses your current income is still not enough to live on, then you need to look at part-time employment. The type of work may not be what you want, and it may not pay well. But right now the important thing is to meet your expenses.

Part-time work includes many jobs in the service sector: restaurants, fast-food outlets, retail stores, lawn maintenance services, and service stations. These positions usually don't require much training or education. The companies will be able to train you in a matter of a few hours or a day.

Part-time work can be found by checking newspaper classified listings under the help wanted ads. Many of these jobs are advertised in storefront windows, so an afternoon of pounding the pavement may yield worthwhile employment. And social service agencies and Job Service also post openings on their jobs listings boards.

When you apply for part-time work, ask the manager to spell out your duties, hours, safety regulations, pay, and benefits—just as you would do with a permanent employer. Be sure you fill out the appropriate W-4 and other tax forms. If you have any questions about the legitimacy of the business, contact your local Chamber of Commerce and/or Better Business Bureau. Don't let the problems of a questionable employer become your problems as well.

Work as hard for your part-time employer as you would for a job you loved with a permanent employer. Such efforts will go far to win respect for yourself and a possible future recommendation from your supervisor. Even if the business you work for isn't exactly related to your field(s) of expertise or in line with your goals, you will always learn something new. Also, you can still network for a permanent job with the people you meet.

Another possibility you may consider for part-time or temporary work involves volunteering to work for a company that you would like to work for permanently. If you can swing the finances and your insurance will cover you, offer your skills and services to a business for a week or two. This way, you and the company can check each other out. Some people have been able to turn such volunteer work into a part-time or permanent position.

### Beware of "Contract Labor"

You may have the opportunity to work for a short time—a day or a week—for an employer. The employer will tell you that you will be paid as "contract labor." You may be tempted to take this short-term and/or part-time work for some fast bucks. Don't do it until after you have answered some important questions. This "contract labor" may be a violation of Internal Revenue Service regulations. It also may be in violation of your state employment regulations.

Consider the following when the opportunity for "contract labor" arises: Are you truly an independent contractor? Or is your employer trying to avoid paying Social Security, workers' compensation, and unemployment insurance taxes on your services? Just because the employer says that you are an "independent contract laborer" doesn't necessarily mean that you are.

If you are an independent contractor doing "contract labor," you should be able to answer yes to the following questions:

☞ Do you have the final responsibility for all business decisions, and how the job will be performed?
☞ Is your business subject to a profit or loss?
☞ Do you declare this profit or loss on your tax returns?
☞ Do you submit bids for the services you will perform?
☞ Is each contract for a specific project?
☞ Do you supply all tools and materials to complete the project?
☞ Are you required to meet the licensing and regulatory requirements of your occupation?
☞ Could you be liable for damages?
☞ Do you guarantee your work?

If you present yourself as an independent contractor and you do this particular work for others, chances are that you are a legitimate independent contractor. This seems obvious, but you should consider what happens when you are unemployed and someone offers you a job that's different from your usual line of work. For example, if you are a salesperson, and a business wants you to paint an office, you would be considered an employee of that business and not an independent (painter) contractor.

These employment regulations are for your own protection. The person who wants to use your services is required to comply with the law. Make sure that you are not cheating yourself. Contact the appropriate federal or state agencies if you have further questions.

TEMPORARY WORK
Temporary work is full-time employment for a period of time less than what you want in a permanent position. For example, retail stores and

tourist industries, such as ski resorts, hire holiday or seasonal help. Also, many unemployed people with a college education seek temporary substitute teaching jobs (depending on state and local requirements for certification).

Temporary service contractors do the lion's share of filling the positions. They've grown from their early role of placing "warm bodies" as assembly line workers in smokestack industries. Now, these contractors supply workers for more white-collar than blue-collar jobs. They connect temporary employees with companies' needs for skilled office and industrial staff for selected projects or to replace employees on sick leave or vacation. These contractors include Kelly Temporary Services, Manpower Temporary Services, and Olsten Temporary Services. Look under "employment contractors" in the Yellow Pages of your telephone book for the agencies in your area.

You may have used the services of these contractors before when you needed flexible hours, extra income for changing family needs, or to cover college expenses. Now you may need the help of the contractors to reconnect you with the working world. Besides the income, temporary employment can provide:

☞ In-depth training, flexibility, and skills enhancement.
☞ Experience to bolster your résumé.
☞ Greater awareness of available job opportunities.
☞ Access to job listings in the companies you work for.

There also is a good chance that temporary employment may result in permanent employment. Gretchen Decker of Manpower Temporary Services said that as many as one-third of its temporary workers are hired full-time by the companies they work for.

If you decide to use a temporary services contractor, keep these important considerations in mind:

1. *Steer clear of contractors that charge you a fee for their services.* This is very important. The companies that draw temporary employees from the contractors pay the contractors to do the recruiting. It's foolish for you, an unemployed person, to pay money to offer your labor to make money.

2. *Look for contractors that care enough to find out who you are.* The best contractors will test you to determine what you enjoy doing and identify your skills and talents. This way, they can make the best

match with you and a prospective company. Contractors that don't care what you can do and place you anyway or anywhere probably don't care what the companies will pay you, either.

3. *Look for contractors that offer up-to-date and hands-on training.* It's in both the contractor's and your own self-interest to make sure you stay sharp in your skills, especially with computer and other high-tech equipment.

4. *Look for contractors that offer fair wages and benefits, such as paid holidays, vacation pay, bonuses, and insurance.* Have the contractors' representatives clearly spell out your pay, benefits, rights, and responsibilities.

Finally, if you choose to seek employment through a temporary services contractor, prepare yourself as if you were looking for a full-time position. You can never get enough practice in interviewing and presenting yourself professionally. The following tips can help you for both temporary and full-time work:

☞ Know what you want in a job and what you are willing to learn.

☞ Make a good first impression through your dress and attitude.

☞ Keep your résumé current and know your work history.

☞ Ask the contractor if you need to prepare for any skills-assessment tests and training.

## SELF-EMPLOYMENT

Hugh's story at the beginning of this chapter is not unusual. Many people who were laid off or fired reason, "If the company that I've given ten years of my life to at forty-plus hours a week wasn't able to care for me, maybe I ought to be my own boss." Some of the greatest success stories in business began with that very attitude. Many small businesses succeed. But many fail.

A company functions because it divides the labor among its employees so it can make a profit. Someone does the designing, another keeps the books, another does the manufacturing—on down the line with quality control, marketing, and sweeping up. When you are self-employed, you do it all. Those who best adapt to self-employment usually have a skill that they can readily market, and are willing to do all the other tasks necessary to keep their business functioning.

Many unemployed persons gradually drift into self-employment. They pick up solo part-time work as they continue their job search for permanent employment with a company or institution. Accountants, computer programmers, and engineers become consultants. Teachers tutor or start their own child-care facilities. Mechanics pick up odd jobs here and there, and soon have a full schedule of customers.

**Check Your Entrepreneurial Quotient**
The most effective self-employed persons are the ones who have done a lot of soul-searching. Once they have figured out what they can and want to do, they zealously pursue their goals without calling it quits after forty hours that week. The U.S. Small Business Administration and the Colorado Department of Labor and Employment suggest that would-be self-employed persons know how to answer these important questions:

☞ Do I have the "entrepreneurial spirit," with its necessary independence, ambition, enthusiasm, creativity, organization, discipline, assertiveness, and willingness to do just plain hard work?
☞ Do I have adequate capital to stay afloat financially long enough for the business to pay off?
☞ Why do I want to do this?
☞ Do I have something I can sell?
☞ Can I produce my own product, or will I act as an intermediary between the manufacturer and the market?
☞ Who or what is the market?
☞ Can I guarantee the product?
☞ Do I have a plan to carry out this business?
☞ Can I afford it? How will I finance it?
☞ Will I need help (a partner or partners)?
☞ Can I risk it? Am I emotionally strong enough to handle the stress and uncertainty of self-employment?
☞ Can I focus all my attention on my self-employment without harming my relationships with my spouse, children, or friends?
☞ Is this venture in line with my long-range goals?

The feasibility of going into business for yourself has grown exponentially because of the revolution in home office equipment—

personal computers, printers, fax machines, photocopiers, and the like. But don't delude yourself into thinking that buying three thousand dollars of equipment will create an "If I buy it, the business will come" reality. No amount of equipment can substitute for a marketable idea, hard work, self-discipline, and long hours. Besides, if you're unemployed, you need to make quite sure that you can afford such an investment.

## Franchises

The proliferation of corporations selling franchises has also spurred the growth of self-employment. Franchised businesses include: food services, cosmetics, investments, real estate, cleaning services, tele-marketing, and mass-mailing operations.

These franchises typically require an initial investment of several thousand to several hundred thousand dollars. The parent company usually provides the product(s) and the list(s) of clients. You provide the muscle and legwork. Many people have done well financially with these businesses.

However, you need to be very, very careful if you decide to buy into a franchise. First, you must know in your heart if this is what you really want to do. Second, you must discover if the franchise is above board. Review its financial statements, company history, and goals. Check with local professionals in the same line of work, the Chamber of Commerce, Better Business Bureau, and your state's attorney general to verify the viability and legality of the franchise. Third, *can you afford it?* Your money is already tight because of your unemployment. Spending it on a franchise could be financially disastrous. Fourth, if you don't like the business, can you get out of it without substantial losses?

## Check the Regulations

Just because you're self-employed doesn't mean nobody except you and your customers are interested. Local, state, and federal governments will be very interested. Before starting any business, make sure that you have your legal and accounting bases covered. The U.S. Small Business Administration suggests that you consider these important requirements:

☞ Internal Revenue Service rules about income and expense reporting.
☞ City and/or county business licenses.
☞ Local zoning regulations.

☞ Bonding licenses.
☞ State seller's licenses.
☞ Sales tax numbers.
☞ Public health regulations.
☞ Incorporation statements.
☞ Federal Employer Identification number(s).

## Records Are Your Responsibility

Remember, the self-empowerment you gain by becoming self-employed has its share of responsibilities. If you are serious about pursuing your dreams as a self-employed person, you must be serious in dealing with your taxes. If you are getting started as a self-employed person, apply these tax tips.

*Keep records of everything.* If you are truly "self-employed," you must show a profit in three of five years (otherwise your "self-employment" is really a hobby), according to the IRS. Profits and losses, therefore, can be proven only by the records you maintain.

Records include: milage and travel expenses, postage, office supplies, publications, legal and professional fees, business seminars, phone bills in which you clearly define which calls were for business and which were personal, times you met with clients, and receipts for everything from business lunches to equipment purchases. The IRS has several ways by which you may deduct purchases and depreciation of home office equipment. Medical insurance and expenses may be deductible as well.

Of course, keep records of all income and reimbursements for expenses. If you earn income from several kinds of self-employment, be sure to keep those accounts separate.

Be very, very careful about declaring your home work area a "home office." Unless you can clearly prove that your "home office" is used for nothing but business (no games with the kids, no place to conduct personal correspondence, and so forth), you are begging for a tax audit. The IRS and some municipal governments have strict rules about what qualifies as a home office. Check with them for their specific guidelines.

Also, don't forget to file the quarterly estimated tax payments for self-employed persons using Form 1040-ES. You can obtain these forms by calling the IRS. In all of these matters, be sure to consult a reputable tax-preparer and be prepared with your records.

These requirements, regulations, tax notifications, and other legal matters are more than petty bureaucratic hassles. They are imperative if you want to protect your finances and reputation. If you have questions about these, contact the Internal Revenue Service, your lawyer and/or accountant, and the U.S. Small Business Administration (SBA) Office of Business Development.

The SBA and your state department of labor and employment publish numerous pamphlets and booklets to help you get started. Look in the government pages of your telephone book for the appropriate numbers.

### HARD WORK AND HARD LUCK

You've probably heard people tell you, "Losing my job was the best thing that ever happened to me." Many of these formerly unemployed people have either found full-time work with a company after doing part-time or temporary work, or they started their own business. They survived and even flourished.

However, perhaps you haven't had it so good. Unemployment hasn't been the jolt you needed to seek another career. Instead, it was the straw that broke your financial back. You aren't concerned about working out of your home because you are about to watch it go into foreclosure. At this point, you are at the end of your rope—and need help fast. Read on.

# CHAPTER FIFTEEN

# When You're at the End of Your Rope

❖

T he premise of much of this book is that you've had one career for a long time. So when you lose your job, most things are fairly well in place. You will still endure a struggle, even a hard struggle. But the safety nets are strong. You have family and friends to support you, maybe even a nest egg for the rainy day that's showering on you.

But perhaps this profile doesn't fit your picture. Perhaps you do not possess the structures that many others take for granted. You may have had personal difficulties that, despite all your efforts, tore your life apart. Many of those difficulties revolve around family life: marriage, children, separation, and divorce. Other more extreme circumstances—crime, violence, illness, or difficulties in caring for an elderly relative—may have put you on a shaky foundation. And it's possible that you were wealthy and stable but lost it all in a bad investment or business deal.

Also, you may not have had a steady career. For one reason or another, it may have taken you a long time to earn your education. Or perhaps you made a career change in mid-life and had to start at the bottom of the corporate ladder along with those in their early twenties. You worked at low-paying jobs with minimal benefits. Consequently, saving for the future wasn't even a possibility. A retirement or pension plan—not to mention investments—was out of the question.

HANGING ON TO THE END OF YOUR ROPE, BY A THREAD

If you are in this position—especially if your unemployment insurance benefits have expired or are about to expire—the consequences of unemployment can get critical—fast. In other words, you could very quickly come to the end of your rope for support systems, cash, shelter, food, and clothing. If you are in this situation, it is imperative that you seek out charitable organizations, social service agencies, and networking possibilities *now*. It's that much more imperative to talk to your landlord, your creditors, and your lenders. Above all, *don't lose hope*. This agonizing time *will* come to an end.

## Crunch Time

When your life is caught in a very serious crunch, you literally may not know where your next meal is coming from. There are some things you should do first if you are facing impending poverty:

1. Cut out *everything* you can. Sort through your possessions and sell everything but the necessities at a garage sale. However, don't pawn items if possible. You will still have to pay the pawnbroker on a monthly basis, and the interest you pay is exorbitant.
2. Although you run the risk of damaging your credit rating, consider stopping payment on all your credit cards, with the exception of ten dollars a month. Your basic issue is to keep food on the table.
3. Delay paying insurance premiums as long as possible. If you believe you can drop the coverage without serious damage to your health, do so.
4. Notify your relatives and closest friends that you may be facing the loss of your home or apartment. You may need their help later, and you don't want to surprise them.
5. Notify your church, social service agency, or other community organization of the same things. The more you tell them, the more they can help you.

## Resist, Resist, Resist

When you face desperate times, you may seek desperate solutions, from crime to suicide. These are very poor and damaging choices. People who under normal circumstances would never filch a piece of candy consider committing crimes when they are unemployed. It is also very easy to succumb to personal temptations of affairs or substance abuse, just because they make you feel good and help you forget your pain for a time.

You may even contemplate suicide, which might become your greatest temptation. Resist suicide with everything you've got. *Get help immediately.* Your church, social service agency, local mental health association, or other community organization can offer counseling.

Resist the temptation to steal. Shoplifting, even for a loaf of bread, will cause you far more short- and long-term problems with the law than any hassles with constantly asking the local social service agency for help. Also, resist the temptation to falsify the information you give to the social service agency. They will find out if you're lying, which will hurt your chances for further assistance.

THE BASICS

Although you must never lose sight of your long-term goals of career and employment, your immediate needs will mean making daily decisions about food, clothing, transportation, health care, utilities, and shelter. They will be painful for you and your family, but they also will help you keep your sanity during a very trying period.

## Food

Food, obviously, is the most critical issue you will have to deal with. Fortunately, of all the needs you have, finding sources of food will be the easiest struggle to overcome. The secret is to know where to look and not be ashamed.

☞ Take advantage of every food give-away program you can find through community organizations and churches.

☞ Eat meals at community agencies or shelters.

☞ Apply for food stamps. Don't give up trying.

☞ If you have children, apply for Aid to Families with Dependent Children (AFDC) and school meal programs.

☞ Strongly resist going to the grocery store. When you must go, buy only the basic necessities. Buy generics. Use coupons.

If you've been working with a social service organization or charity, they may be able to pull some strings and help you out with other food distribution programs.

## Clothing

You're in a good situation if you need clothes, too. Most thrift shops run by social service agencies and churches, and especially stores such as

Goodwill, will have enough clothing to get you through at least several months. Make clothes last as long as you can. You already know that staying in style is a luxury you can't afford.

## Transportation

This is more difficult to arrange than food or clothing.

If you live in an urban area with public transportation, you must consider selling your car. That's a harsh move, because the car is often a necessary tool for the job hunt and taking care of family necessities. But if selling the car means that you can raise quick cash or eliminate monthly payments (as well as expenses for insurance, fuel, and maintenance), you have that much more money for food and rent.

Of course, if you have two cars, immediately sell the one that will give you the most money or save you the most cash in payments, insurance, and maintenance.

If public transportation is minimal or not available, you may need to borrow a car from a friend. Make sure that you and the car are covered by insurance. A social service agency may offer transportation so you can buy groceries or travel to an interview.

## Health Care

This will be difficult, too. The stress of unemployment, poor diet, long hours, and exposure to the elements will lower your resistance to disease. Basic medical care, such as routine physicals, may be hard to find. But you cannot neglect yourself if you get sick. That will intensify the other effects of stress. A disease could spread to the rest of your family. And it will frustrate your job hunt.

Ask your social service agency if any low-cost health clinics operate in your area, especially clinics offering services for children. Many large cities have universities with medical schools, which in turn operate clinics. Use a hospital emergency room only as a last resort. And remember that many doctors still offer treatment on a sliding-fee basis.

## Utilities

Early in your unemployment, see if your utility company has a program to cover utility payments for the poor and elderly. You may be able to qualify for assistance with your bills. If you are facing foreclosure or eviction, your utilities will be shut off anyway. Until that time comes, observe these precautions to keep costs down:

☞ Turn the air conditioner off and keep it off.

☞ Keep on only enough heat to prevent the pipes from freezing. You can bundle up or spend your days at the library.

☞ Keep water use to a minimum.

☞ The telephone is critical for your job search. But you may need to disconnect it if none of your leads has panned out. Ask neighbors or relatives if you can use their phones. Keep the calls to a bare minimum, and make every effort to barter your labor as a means of payment. Some social service agencies will take messages for you and allow you to use their phones.

Shutting off your utilities is an extreme measure. It always will cost you cash for security deposits and start-up fees later when you need to reconnect them. But missing payments and then having the utility company shut off utilities for you is worse. Then you've not only saddled yourself with deposits and fees later on, but also damaged your valuable credit rating—which will cost you more in the long run.

## HOME, SHAKY HOME: WHEN YOU FEAR YOU WILL LOSE YOUR HOUSE OR APARTMENT

Of all the end-of-your-rope concerns, shelter will be your most expensive and problematic issue. "Home" is more than four walls and a roof. It represents safety, family, warmth, a place of refuge, "the American dream," and a base for work or seeking work.

### If You Own a House

Your house is your most valuable asset. The prospect of losing it is a serious emotional as well as a financial hardship. If you have trouble or anticipate trouble making your payments, you are at serious risk of losing your home to foreclosure. *If you do nothing, you will lose your home.*

Sue Davies, a Certified Housing Counselor with the Consumer Credit Counseling Service of Southern Colorado, explained that the consequences of foreclosure are serious and long-term:

☞ Foreclosure doesn't end your relationship with your house. If it is sold at a public auction for less than what you owe on it—called the "deficiency balance"—the mortgage company or insuring/guaranteeing agency may attempt to collect that difference from you.

☞ If your home is guaranteed through the Department of Veterans Affairs (VA), you may not be able use your VA eligibility in other areas until any debt is repaid.

☞ Foreclosure can affect your taxes when the deficiency balance is forgiven. That amount will be reported to the IRS as income. You will be taxed on that income. This could amount to thousands of dollars, which you cannot afford when you are out of work.

☞ Although not as bad as bankruptcy, a foreclosure will be listed on your credit record for seven years. Such a negative listing may affect your ability to obtain credit cards and consumer loans.

☞ It will also hurt your job hunt. Prospective employers often conduct credit checks on prospective employees, especially for jobs requiring a security clearance.

☞ Family relationships may be strained to the breaking point because of the financial hardships and the stress of moving.

☞ Your foreclosed house will negatively affect the values of your neighbors' homes.

Sue Davies also explained that foreclosure processes and timetables vary from state to state. They also differ depending on the kind of loan you have, such as a VA, FHA (Federal Housing Administration), or CV (Conventional) loan. Each of these variables has specific alternatives to foreclosure. They aren't necessarily easy; some require financial sacrifice. Alternatives include:

*Refinancing.* This includes any loan restructuring—such as rewriting the loan at a lower interest rate or for a longer period of time—so you can continue to make payments compatible with your financial situation.

*Loan to reinstate.* This is a loan from any source—friends, insurance policies or retirement plans, credit unions—that can be applied to the back payments, penalties, and other delinquent costs.

*Selling your home.* This action is risky because you are under a lot of pressure, you don't have much room to negotiate, and you may take a loss. Even a loss, however, will avoid the negative effect of a foreclosure. Use a real estate agent who is familiar with selling homes nearing foreclosure.

*Deed-in-lieu of foreclosure.* Sometimes a mortgage lender will allow the homeowner to deed the property back to them in place of paying off the mortgage. The homeowner loses all equity, incurs a seven-year negative on his or her credit report, and may be liable to continuing liability—that is, the homeowner may have to agree to pay for all or part of the difference of the total debt and the net proceeds of the sale.

*Forbearance agreements*. This agreement between the homeowner and lender enables the homeowner to make up late payments. These work well if your period of unemployment has been brief and you have maintained a good history of making payments.

*HUD assignment*. You may be able to work out an arrangement with your lender in which the Department of Housing and Urban Development (HUD) takes over your loan, enabling you to suspend or reduce your payments. This is a complicated program, so stay in close contact with your mortgage company.

*VA alternatives*. There are a variety of programs through which the VA pays the lender for an outstanding loan amount and then restructures the loan; provides financial assistance to the veteran to sell the home; arranges to accept the deed from the homeowner in a deed-in-lieu of foreclosure; or arranges to reduce the current interest rate on the mortgage.

*Short payoff*. This happens when your sell the home without receiving enough to pay off the entire mortgage. Private mortgage insurance, a VA compromise agreement, or a pre-foreclosure sale by a homeowner with an FHA loan may be able to help you through this obligation.

If there is *any* possibility that your house may go into foreclosure, *seek help immediately*. As discussed earlier, the best prevention for a foreclosure is to stay in close contact with your lender. Foreclosure is trouble for your lender, too. Any and all help you can give them will help you as well.

Also, contact the Consumer Credit Counseling Service nearest you. If you don't know of one, call their national hot-line at 1-800-388-2227 (as of book publication date).

Contact a HUD-approved housing counseling agency. Their services will be free for housing counseling. Go as soon as you can. There are more options if you get into it early in the game. Know what the foreclosure process is in your state, and determine how much time you have. Know your rights as a homeowner. And make copies of all documents.

Beware of scams that target those in danger of losing their homes. So-called "foreclosure counselors" or fly-by-night lenders can take advantage of your vulnerability and cheat you out of thousands of dollars in "processing fees" or even cheat you out of your house. Seek advice from the Better Business Bureau, your lender, or a Consumer Credit Counseling Service if you have *any* questions about the credibility of someone who promises an easy way out.

Holding on to your home through your unemployment will be a major victory for you, now and for the future. Don't give up.

*If it all falls through* and your lender has made the decision to foreclose, the best decision you can make is to stay in the house until you are about to be evicted. It sounds cynical, but at least you're getting free rent for that short period (depending on how quickly foreclosure proceedings occur in your state). You still must face that day, however, when you will sleep in a place other than what you called home.

### Renting

If you rent, you won't be hit with as many hassles as losing a house. However, you still face the basic issue of where you will live.

The best way to avoid eviction is to stay in touch with your landlord and pay what you can. If you've faithfully paid your rent in the past, you have built a reputation that may help you negotiate some time, if not delay rent payments. Ask your landlord if there is any way he can apply the deposit you paid on the apartment toward a month's rent.

If you can find a cheaper apartment, and especially if you can move to a cheaper apartment in the same building or complex, you must consider moving. That way, you protect your references for future housing. One address over a long period shows that you are a stable tenant. You also eliminate or reduce the stress and headaches involved in moving to another address.

However, if you haven't been able to pay the rent for several months, or your landlord won't tolerate you missing or reducing the rent for even a month, you must deal with eviction. When you realize this will happen, begin to pack your belongings. But wait to leave until the last possible day.

### Where to Go

If you are evicted, you have several options. Most communities have a shelter of some sort. Ask a social service agency, a church, a YMCA, or other community organization where you can go.

The facilities may be crowded and without much privacy, but at least you'll sleep in a bed, eat a hot meal, and possibly be able to take a shower. As the number of homeless families has increased in recent years, so has the number of shelters for those families.

If you can move in with relatives, make arrangements to do so. The sooner you can let them know, the better. You are already experiencing tremendous stress. Showing up on your brother's doorstep unannounced will simply exacerbate the tension while putting more stress on the relationship, especially if you are bringing a family with you. If you want to move in with out-of-town relatives, you must weigh the costs of moving your possessions or placing them in storage.

You may be able to move in with friends, or make arrangements to stay with friends on a rotating basis. Take along only the minimal amount of possessions you need to live.

The toughest part about seeking shelter with relatives, and especially with friends, is when you need them to take care of your children in order for you to hunt for work out of the area. Be willing to swap baby-sitting time.

Regardless of whether you move in with friends or relatives, realize that you are a guest. This situation will be hard on all of you. Their hospitality gives you no right to abuse any of the privileges—food, heat, telephone, and so forth—they will share. Show friends or relatives that you are serious and want your stay to be pleasant and short by actively seeking work.

At this point, you don't have the luxury of mulling over career options. You will need to take whatever work you can find in order to start your life anew. In the meantime, you should offer to barter your time: wash the dishes, clean the house or apartment, shop for the food, and take care of their children.

The time will fast approach when you need something more permanent than staying in a shelter or with family and friends. Ask your church, community center, or social service agency about available low-income housing in your area.

## DON'T GIVE UP

You may not be able to see the end of this agonizing phase now, but it will come. Even though you won't know how long it will last, when you cry out, *Will this ever be over with?* you can rest in the hope that the answer is yes.

Don't give up. Don't give in to the temptations that offer fleeting comfort or permanent self-destruction. Don't lose sight of the fact that many people care for you, love you, and want to see you survive and succeed. Your perseverance is an inspiration to others.

Finally, keep your dignity. You are a child of God. You are not a government statistic, a bum, or a helpless person. Don't let others put you down. Even when everything else is out of control, you can control how you take care of yourself. Stand up straight, smile, and look others in the eye. You will survive.

# III

## "Where Do I Go from Here?"

—

## The Road Back to Employment

# CHAPTER SIXTEEN

# Developing a Focus

Y our self-esteem lies in the gutter. Your personal relationships are strained. And your financial situation registers desperate. Unemployment is the Mohave Desert of working life. While you're picking sand out of your teeth, the last thing you want to do is meet your situation head-on, put on a cheerful face, and go look for a job.

From the moment you heard that you would lose your job, your overriding concerns were: "What will I do next? What will be my next job? Where will I go? Can I survive?" All the techniques and skills offered in this book for coping with unemployment are designed to smooth the rough spots during your search for new employment, if not a new career. Unemployment gives you time to take inventory of who you are and what you want. People who are steadily employed often roll through life without ever seriously considering these issues—to the detriment of their own fulfillment and happiness. However, unemployment isn't necessarily the best time to do serious career planning because you're so intent on surviving and pulling in enough cash to pay the bills.

But if surviving unemployment is like wandering through a desert, hunting for a new job is like hacking your way through the Amazon rain forest. But don't start wielding a machete if you don't know where you want to go.

## WELCOME TO THE JOB HUNT JUNGLE
When you're trying to blaze a trail to a new job, it's easy to be overwhelmed by the dense undergrowth of hundreds of books, articles,

seminars, videos, and audio presentations in libraries and bookstores, on television and the radio—covering everything from résumé and cover letter writing to interviewing and negotiating a job offer. All of these materials have something worthwhile to offer. But when you are unemployed, they all seem to blur together.

What follows in the next four chapters is a method that has worked for many people, a method different from what people often use for conventional job hunting. For this method, I am deeply indebted to Neil Duppen, a Denver-area career counselor with extensive experience in human resource management. He has written hundreds of job descriptions and developed salary structures for major corporations. He also has led a job support group at the Cherry Hills Community Church since the mid-1980s.

Neil has developed a simple system for career counseling and job hunting. But that doesn't necessarily mean that it's easy. You need to make the commitment to work through the process. No book or advisor—regardless of promises—can do your career and job searching for you. After all, no books or advisors will do your job for you. Nor will they pick up your paycheck.

You have essentially two different methods to find a job. The conventional way is to find out what jobs are out there. You sample the variety of available careers and use the definitions of those jobs as your reference point(s). You scan the help-wanted ads in the paper, talk to a career counselor, ask friends, and pore over the reference books in the library. (For a mind-numbing experience, look through the tens of thousands of career specialties in the U.S. Department of Labor's *Dictionary of Occupational Titles* and *The Occupational Outlook Handbook*.) After you've blitzed your brain doing this, you try to craft a résumé to fit the job and farm yourself out to the company that's offering it.

This method has worked for many people. There's a perceived security in responding to an ad or having someone tell you what's out there. But there are problems with this method. First, there is no way that you can get a handle on everything that's available. Second, you're playing the same game and competing with millions of other players. Third, even if you had a fair chance of competing, you are taking a gamble every time you send out a résumé or make a phone call. You can't present yourself well enough to meet the demands of each and every job and/or company. Fourth, and most important, the whole process is external to who you are, simply because you spend little time focusing on yourself and proceeding accordingly.

WHO ARE YOU?—PART TWO

If the method just described doesn't work, or at the least is really frustrating, would you consider method number two? This method starts by asking the question "Who am I?" and working toward a conclusion. It is grounded on the very basic principle that was discussed in chapter 8: You are a valuable person, and your talents, skills, and hopes are expressions of what God created you to be.

Start with your heart—your loves and desires. Then the career, job, satisfaction, and money will follow. This is the practical side of healing your damaged self-esteem and then pressing forward. And when you've got hope and a direction, others can help you more effectively.

One of the saddest statements a person can utter at the close of a lifetime is, "I wish I could have . . ." or "I always wanted to. . . ." Many people are trapped by oppressive political or social systems and are never able to exercise their full potential. But if we have the freedom, it's nothing short of a sin to go to our graves wishing for things that we could have done. That is why unemployment can be a blessing in disguise: It's a wake-up call. Painful circumstances have grabbed our attention, shaken us, and yelled at us, "Okay, pal, who are you? What do you want, and how will you go about finding it?"

Neil Duppen guides people through a four-step process of thinking based on this second method. Each of these steps is part of a continuum. None can be isolated from the other. And all center on your ability to respond to the request: "Tell me about yourself." The four steps are:

1. *Being focused*—explaining your strengths and what you want with excitement.
2. *The résumé*—after you have focused your strengths and wants, you can create the document that succinctly tells others about yourself.
3. *Networking*—interacting with people who can help you find what you want.
4. *Interviewing*—the threshold of connecting what you want with the people and/or company who can give it to you.

## CHANGING YOUR THINKING

The simple but industrious tasks of focusing—finding out who you are and what you want—will take time. But before you dive into those exercises, you should realize that you will need to do more than simply draw up a few lists and answer a few questions. What you will need—and this is hard during unemployment—is what is sometimes referred to as making a "paradigm shift": a change in the way you think. Others can offer suggestions, but they can't change you, just as you can't change them.

To understand this better, consider these popular brain-teasers. You've probably seen this diagram, or something like it, with the request that you identify what it is. It looks like a vase, but it also

portrays the silhouettes of two profiles facing each other. You sense your brain shifting back and forth, trying to decide which image it sees. You are experiencing a paradigm shift.

Or consider this puzzle of three rows of three dots. Put a pencil down on any dot, and without picking it up, draw four continuous straight lines to connect all the dots. (You may want to try this on a piece of paper before you look at the solution on page 214.)

●　　●　　●

●　　●　　●

●　　●　　●

(Hint: If you perceive there is a box, and that you can't draw the lines beyond the boundaries of the dots, you can't solve the puzzle. However, solving the puzzle is not as important as grasping the whole process. The point is, how do you perceive yourself and the puzzles you face?)

The task of focusing, as in the working world, means that you need to break out of "boxes." For example, if you think that age will work against you in looking for a particular job or career, you've made a box for yourself. Or if you don't believe there's any opportunity in a given profession or trade, that's what you'll find.

How you perceive yourself is critical to how others will perceive you. If you see yourself "boxed" in, others have no reason not to box you in, either. That's why you start your focus step by looking at your strengths.

## MAKING A STRENGTHS LIST

The first task in becoming focused—which will directly affect your résumé, networking, and interviewing—is to take a sheet of paper and list your strengths. You may have seen checklists of skills that seem to do the same thing. But there is a subtle but crucial difference between that and writing down your strengths yourself. A checklist is passive. At best, it requires little thinking on your part. At the worst, it boxes you into what the composer of the checklist thinks is important.

A blank sheet of paper is a frightening thing. But here's where you apply your ability to change your way of thinking. This exercise involves more than writing "I can type," although you might jot that down. It's an assessment of the talents, skills, training, and desires you possess. So start brainstorming:

☞ What do I like to do?
☞ What am I good at doing?
☞ What makes me feel good after I've done it?
☞ What do others compliment me for? (This is an outside opinion, and as long as it's constructive, it can benefit you.)
☞ How have I defined myself in my working life, social life, personal life, and other ways?

Don't stop with these ideas. And don't stop to analyze each item you've written down. You'll have time for that later. The objective here is to stretch your mind and have fun. This is worth taking time for, and it will save you immense time in the future.

After you've worked on this list for several hours or several days, bounce your findings off your spouse or a friend. Continue to flesh out the strengths you've found, and continue to write down what you've discovered during your brainstorming. You probably will find things about yourself that you only suspected but never really considered. You are learning who you are. You are learning self-empowerment.

As exciting as this is, you may hear a nasty little voice whisper in your ear, "Write down your weaknesses, too." *Don't do it.* There's a whole world out there eager to tell you what you're no good at. You may have had peers, parents, or other authority figures in your past tell you that you were incompetent or even worse. In turn, you may have conditioned yourself to be open to this self-destructive mentality. Unless you have a stadium-sized ego, you already know what your weaknesses are. Your unemployment has only reinforced them. This exercise of writing down your strengths is intended to break you out of that way of thinking—that box—so you can start moving in a healthy direction. And the next step in that direction entails another list—namely, what you want in a job.

## MAKING A JOB CHARACTERISTICS LIST

After you've written your strengths list, get another sheet of paper and write down what you want in a job. Okay, so it's not as easy as "low hours, high pay, nice bosses, five-week vacations—and an office with a view." But in your more realistic and sober moments, you do think about what you really want to do, in what context you'd like to do it, and even how much you'd like to get paid for it.

The problem is that you most likely let these fleeting thoughts zip through your mind and vanish into the mists of day-to-day activity. You don't think about them much until you're forced to—such as when you're unemployed. You even may have considered some of these issues if you considered part-time or temporary work or self-employment.

This list, too, means brainstorming. The process is similar to what you did with the strengths list. But keep in mind this caution: Don't try to harmonize this list with the strengths list. They may or may not match. That's not important at this point. What *is* important is to get your desires out in the open and down on paper. Start, but don't end, with the following questions:

☞ What do I want to do?

☞ What values are important to me in my employment and in the company and/or people I work for?

☞ Do I want to work with people or by myself?

☞ Do I want an indoor job, an outdoor job, or a combination?

☞ What are the opportunities for advancement?

☞ Do I want to travel?

☞ Where do I want to live and/or do business?

☞ What size company (sales, employees, variety of products) do I want to work for?

☞ Finally, what is my minimum salary requirement?

As with the strengths list, you'll probably hear another nasty little voice whisper in your ear, "That's what you *want* to do—what about what you *can't* or *don't* want to do?" Again, you already have the rest of the world or your own fears telling you what you can't or don't want to do. You won't be able to define what you want realistically by listing what you *don't* want. Companies don't hire employees for what they can't or don't want to do, either. So stomp on every thought that teases, "I don't want to work nights" and so forth. Be drawn toward your desires instead of being pushed away from what you fear or don't think you can do.

## REFINING STRENGTHS AND JOB CHARACTERISTICS

What started as a couple of blank sheets of paper has blossomed into personal insights and desires regarding who you are. Exciting, isn't it? No one else can do this for you. Remember the employment scams discussed in chapter 13? Many of them are successful because the scam artists prey on the unprepared job hunter's failure to focus on knowing who he or she is. The scam artists are doing your focusing for you—and fleecing you in the process.

### I Get Confused with a Little Help from My Friends

Now that you have established these lists, start refining them. Otherwise, you will know a little about your strengths and desired job characteristics, but not enough to know what to do with them. If you stay general, you'll put yourself in the same box as other people do. At that point, people try to help—with minimal if not detrimental results. Friends and family will offer all sorts of suggestions because you've found—if only vaguely—who you are and what you want to do. You will spin your career wheels because they're pumping the accelerator. It's only after you know who you are and what you want that your friends can help you substantially.

The next step is to *get specific*. For example, if you wrote that you are good at "managing money" in the strength list, analyze and refine it. How have you managed money before? Where? For what firm? What challenges or obstacles did you face? How did you overcome them? What were the results? Did you enjoy it?

As you continue refining the lists, you will begin to see connections between them. Sometimes those connections aren't visible at first. For example, you may have written in the "job characteristics" list that you want to work outdoors in a wilderness. You may have had such a desire before but dismissed it because it seemed to have nothing to do with your strength of "managing money." That's because you may have always thought that "managing money" was done in a downtown office or over power lunches.

Now you again sense the paradigm shifts you experienced when you reflected on the puzzles earlier in the chapter. Other connections will begin to surface. You may think, "Wait a minute, no one ever said that I *can't* apply a strength to something I love."

This is when you can profitably begin to consult reference books such as *The Dictionary of Occupational Titles* to see which jobs may fit your newfound connections. The problem with looking at such a reference work before you've done this focusing is that you may miss these connections. You also can review trade journals and seek out people's advice now because you know what you want in ways that would have been unthinkable before you started refining your strengths and job characteristics.

Refining also means editing yourself. Just because you get specific doesn't mean you need to be long-winded. Over time, especially when you start working on your résumé, you will tighten the responses. Be concise. The fewer words you have to say, the better you can write your résumé, the better you can tell people what you want when you network, and the better you can respond in your interview.

THE WHY-YOU-LEFT LIST
While you were brainstorming and completing your lists, you probably heard the ghosts of former employers and coworkers whispering com-

ments about what went wrong at your last job. These are negative if not destructive thoughts. So while you are in this focusing process, deal with them once and for all.

Take a sheet of paper and write out why you were laid off, fired, or otherwise left your former employer. Draw from the diary you kept after you lost your job. Your exit interview will be helpful here, too. Be honest but gentle with yourself. Summarize the chronology of why you left, the key points of disagreement, and how you responded. Be able to give specific examples for each point.

At the end of this exercise, write out several things you learned that made you a better person and will make you a better worker for your next employer. Revise all of these points so you can answer, "Why did you leave your last job?" with certainty, precision, confidence, and lack of animosity.

REEDUCATION AND RETOOLING
One of the most important decisions you will make during your unemployment and job search is if you should go back to school, whether for a refresher course, vocational training, or a college or graduate degree. Reeducation and retooling are lifelong experiences. But they can take place in variety of settings: a classroom, browsing through a library, or walking through the woods or a museum.

No competent doctor would dare consider neglecting the professional literature in his or her specialty just to save time. Patients' lives depend on knowledge of current medical developments. Your own life depends on keeping your knowledge and skills sharp. The global economy has become so competitive that techniques and training acquired in the 1970s and 1980s are often being rendered obsolete in the 1990s.

Only two generations ago, a man (usually) would typically be the breadwinner for the family, staying in one or two jobs in one career for life. The average family now has two breadwinners, and they will have many jobs and several careers over the course of a lifetime. Some choose to adapt, some don't. Quite possibly you don't have a choice. If you were laid off along with hundreds or thousands of others, that could be a very good sign that you are in a profession or industry that is evolving, shrinking, or dying. Get rid of the romantic notion that wishing will bring it back.

During unemployment, many people take time to earn an undergraduate or graduate degree. College graduates facing a competitive job market often give up looking and then pursue a graduate degree. This is a good thing—if the students know what they want to do with their lives.

However, Neil Duppen says going back to school can be a way of delaying your decision about what you want to do. A former college instructor himself, Neil urges people first to make a decision about what they want to do with their lives. Otherwise, they'll take a major in college just because some counselor suggests it, or because "it seemed like the right thing to do at the time." Then, after they get out of school, they face the fallout from the financial hardships of paying for their education. And once again, they try to make a decision about what they want to do.

If you have done your focusing and you find that you don't have some of the needed strengths for a job you want, then you may reasonably consider more education. But before you rush over to the local university or community college—and pay for a course with your precious unemployment dollars—think about what it is you want to learn and why. You may be able to find that education for a lot less than you think. Many large temporary employment services offer training on state-of-the-art equipment, and they will find you a position as well. Many churches, community centers, union halls, and high school continuing education programs may also offer the training you need. And, depending on the career or job you want, many companies train their own workers anyway.

## READY FOR THE RÉSUMÉ

With your strengths and job characteristics lists, you know that you are getting close to the mark when you're excited about what you are writing down. Once you know what you want, then you can go find it—or obtain more training to learn how to do it. You are experiencing the paradigm shift. You are learning to focus. You are well on the way to the next phase of looking for a new career and new employment—writing your résumé.

# CHAPTER SEVENTEEN

# Crafting a Résumé

A résumé is your literary way of telling another person about yourself. You conceive it as you list your capabilities in your focus, as you lay out its form and content, and in the ways you use it when you network. As scary as all this sounds, crafting a résumé shouldn't be that difficult—if you've done your homework in your focusing exercises. For some people, writing their résumé is their way of doing their focusing.

The résumé continues focusing with its overarching query, "Tell me about yourself." You can write a résumé without having done the focusing, but you won't be sure if it is what you want. Also, just as no one can do your focusing for you, neither can another person or résumé writing service thoroughly convey what *you* want on a résumé.

Résumé writing receives more attention than most other aspects of job hunting. Scores of good books are available on the topic. Many of these books and guides differ in their philosophies about résumés, so you need to weigh what works best for you. The danger in all this help is that too many suggestions may steer you away from the purpose of a résumé—and the paradox of a résumé as well.

## THE PURPOSE AND PARADOX OF A RÉSUMÉ

The objective of both the résumé and the cover letter that introduces it is to remind those with whom you network of who you are. You also hope a résumé will grab a prospective employer's interest long enough to trigger a call for an interview. You are trying to persuade the prospective employer—often a total stranger—to conclude, "I would like to get to know this person better." In extremely rare cases, the résumé alone is enough to persuade a personnel director or manager to call you and hire you over the phone.

Paradoxically, résumés aren't that effective, especially when you consider your competition—namely the hundreds if not thousands of other job hunters who are using résumés for the same job you want.

## Meet the Competition

You have competition for a job—a lot of competition. Companies in search of just the right person for a particular position must ruthlessly screen the zillions of résumés they receive if they are ever to get to the interviewing and hiring stages.

Human resource managers will often read through hundreds of résumés at one sitting. They take anywhere from thirty seconds to no more than two minutes to read through a cover letter and résumé. Then they place it in one of three piles: "call," "no," or "maybe." Your next job will hinge on the minute (if that much) that the human resource person will spend reading your objective, work history, and qualifications. How well you do your focusing, and then articulate it in your résumé, may be the final push the human resource manager needs to move your résumé from the "maybe" pile to the "call" pile.

If your résumé makes it to the "call" pile, it will then be passed on to other managers for review. This screening process continues until either the résumé is rejected or put in a file or you are invited to the company for an interview.

### RÉSUMÉ STRUCTURE AND CONTENT

There are as many varieties of résumés as there are people looking for jobs. In fact, there are *more* résumés than people looking for jobs, because the same person ideally will be approaching different prospective employers with different résumés.

As you consider the following suggestions, you would do well to consult other books on résumé writing. More important than that, start applying your networking skills by talking with others in the field in which you want to work. Also, speak to personnel directors, human resource managers, and supervisors at companies to discover what they look for.

## Type of Résumé: Reverse Chronological or Functional?

Denver-area career counselor Neil Duppen said you will write one of two types of résumés: reverse chronological or functional.

*Reverse chronological* (see figure 17-1). This type of résumé lists your job history in a reverse chronological order: that is, starting with the most recent job first. These résumés are geared to job hunting in the same field in which you work or have worked. But because this type of résumé emphasizes time, it deemphasizes accomplishments. Even so, if you've done your focusing well, you should be able to specify your accomplishments within each subheading of the firms you worked for.

FIGURE 17-1
EXAMPLE OF A REVERSE CHRONOLOGICAL RÉSUMÉ

Kelley Jackson
333 Pineridge Lane
Whitestone, MT 12345
(460)555-4321

OBJECTIVE:    ADMINISTRATIVE ASSISTANT

EXPERIENCE
Since 1992    Temporary work through Amalgamated Temp Services, Whitestone, Mont. Performed part-time secretarial duties including typing, word processing, and transcribing at Happy Days Child Care Center.

1985–1991    Secretary to the president of Whitestone Quarry and Mining, Whitestone, Mont. Coordinated all executive scheduling. Developed information systems now widely used in other mining companies throughout the state. Drafted forms used at all levels of the company, in addition to typing, word processing, and filing.

1978–1983    Receptionist at Big Tree State University, Greystone, Mont. Took calls, typed letters for administration personnel. Gave guided tours of the campus.

SKILLS    Can run the office for a CEO.
Can overhaul bureaucratic forms and communications.
Adept at desktop publishing.
Type and do word processing.

EDUCATION    Big Tree State University, Greystone, Mont. Bachelor of Science in Geology. Graduated with honors, 1982.
Arrowhead High School, Arrowhead, Mont., 1976.

References available upon request.

Out of full-time work since March 1992, Kelley wants to stay in the same line of work she did since her college years. She finessed the fact that she lost her job after the mining company's president resigned and the new president didn't want her services. She straightforwardly kept the chronology alive by referring to the temporary work she does. The temporary work shows that she took a step down in her career, but was still active. She's not ashamed to show that she could roll with the punches of unemployment.

The reverse chronology served her well as far as her work record, but not her personal life. The missing year, 1984, could be problematic for Kelley. That was the year her marriage fell apart and she moved into a cabin in the mountains to live alone. This gap may be awkward for her to explain to a prospective employer.

*Functional* (see figure 17-2). The functional résumé—emphasizing accomplishments and capabilities—is preferable in most cases to a chronological résumé. This kind of résumé is especially appropriate when you are looking for work that differs from what you have done in the past. Prospective employers can quickly determine whether you will meet their needs. To construct this résumé, you marshal your qualifications and education so they best describe your capabilities. Use headings that stress your capabilities, not when you worked for a particular firm.

### Customize

As best as is possible, customize your résumé for the job you want. A résumé that looks generic and reads like a list of generalizations will be weeded out early simply because you make yourself appear as if you don't know what you want. A résumé doesn't need to be purely reverse chronological or functional, either. If combining the two styles tells your story better than either style alone, by all means do so.

### Should You Include an Objective?

You would do well to ask people in your desired line of work whether they prefer to see objectives stated on résumés. Some advisors suggest that you leave the objective off the résumé because it may unnecessarily eliminate you from consideration.

If you decide to state an objective, look through several résumé books and compare their suggestions for tailoring what you write to the line of work you're seeking. For example, some résumé guides suggest that you write out your objective at the top of the first page of the résumé. This way, you let the reader of the résumé know immediately what you want.

**FIGURE 17-2**
**EXAMPLE OF A FUNCTIONAL RÉSUMÉ**

---

Kelley Jackson
333 Pineridge Lane
Whitestone, MT 12345
(460)555-4321

OBJECTIVE: Reclamation supervisor for a mining company.

QUALIFICATIONS
- In-depth knowledge of the challenges and operations of a mining company.
- Excellent office organization skills.
- Geology and environmental sciences education.
- Skilled at learning new technologies, including anything with personal computers and desktop publishing.

EXPERIENCE
Mining
- Worked as administrative assistant to the president of Whitestone Quarry and Mining, Whitestone, Mont., from 1985–1991. Coordinated all executive scheduling. Developed information systems now widely used in other mining companies throughout the state. Worked with relevant federal and state officials to implement company's reclamation efforts. Drafted forms used at all levels of the company, in addition to typing, word processing, and filing.
- Graduated with honors in Geology with an emphasis in mining from Big Tree State University, Greystone, Mont., 1982. Minored in Environmental Studies.

Outdoors
- Avid hunter, fisher and rock climber.
- Lived in a cabin alone for a year fifty miles from the nearest town. Learned lifelong lessons in self-sufficiency.
- Skilled at driving everything from light trucks to earthmovers.

Other Experience
- Since 1991, temporary work and secretarial duties through Amalgamated Temp Services, Whitestone, Mont.
- 1978–1983, receptionist at Big Tree State University, Greystone, Mont. Gave guided tours of the campus.

References available upon request.

---

This résumé suits Kelley's shift in her career goals. She plays her strengths in what she knows about the mining industry, as well as personal experiences that would have been liabilities had she tried to remain an administrative assistant. Living alone in the woods is now an asset.

## Your Track Record, Not Your Titles

Do not list the positions you have held. A position is a title with a limited definition. Different companies, not to mention different careers, will define even the same position in different ways. Some companies might not have that position, so such a title will be meaningless to the person who reads the résumé. Your position or job title may have been very important with lots of responsibility. But that won't help you in your job search if you don't define it and qualify it with specifics.

Instead, write down your qualifications. List examples of things you have accomplished, and use action verbs to drive your points home. If you were a sales manager, write how much sales increased over a certain period of time. If you were a foreman, tell how many people you supervised and what you built. If you were an engineer, describe the projects you designed.

## Organization

When you organize your résumé, depending on whether it's a reverse chronological or functional résumé, present your greatest strengths first. For example, if you are a recent college or high school graduate, you've spent most of your time on your education. You probably would list that high on your résumé. If you've had part-time jobs that relate directly to the job you apply for, then put those first. However, if you've been in the workforce for a decade or more, then education should be lower in the résumé, even if you went to a prestigious school. Remember, a personnel director and/or supervisor will be taking only a minute or two to read your résumé. So don't bury your strengths at the bottom of the page.

## Dealing with a Firing or Layoff

A layoff, and especially a firing, is one of the diciest things you will deal with in your résumé. Even hinting at a firing is a definite red flag for a prospective employer. You can do yourself great harm if you don't handle this the right way. You certainly never want to mention, "I was fired . . ." especially if you were fired for cause.

Here, it's best to use a functional résumé. This way, the gaps in your work history won't be so obvious. When you do write that you were employed with Corporation X, mention that you worked from one year to another year, list your duties and accomplishments, and leave it at that. You can't help that you are in this situation, but you can control whether you draw attention to it.

If you were laid off as part of a company "downsizing," you're in a much better situation. If the company conducted a public layoff, you can list the dates you worked there. Then gently mention that your position was phased out as part of a company downsizing. Because of the increasingly frequent turnovers at businesses in the global economy, job loss is no longer stigmatized the way it used to be. Employers are well aware that many of the résumés they receive are from people who are out of work through little or no fault of their own.

If you have been out of work for a while, and you have been able to do temporary, consulting, or freelance work in your field, you should list that as your current position. That way, you can state that you worked at a company from date A to date B. After date B you have been working on your own. It lets the prospective employer know that you developed your skills, experience, and career and didn't roll over and die.

## Details, Details

As dear as our personal and family lives are, they don't belong on a résumé. You, not your spouse or children, are the one looking for a job. Some firms prefer married employees and some prefer single employees. Most don't care. But you don't want a company to screen you on issues that are irrelevant to whether you can perform a job.

Additionally, it is illegal for interviewers to ask you about your race, ethnicity, disabilities, religion (except when the company is affiliated with a religion or religious organization), and marital or family status. You can put personal family details on your résumé if you wish. But once you do, don't be surprised if an interviewer wants to hint at or goad you into talking about your family background.

Other details to consider are:

☞ Hobbies, avocations, and sports let the interviewers know that you are a well-rounded person. Many people have included them with successful results. Some employers, however, may regard them as trite or trivial.

☞ Don't include age, height, or weight unless the job requires some sort of physical prowess. Do not include a photo.

☞ References are generally not included on résumés. You can simply write, "References available upon request." An exception to this rule might be if you are sure that the person reading the résumé personally knows your references.

You will be able to find out from networking whether these personal details are relevant on a résumé.

## TIPS ON FORMAT

First impressions count as much on a résumé as they do when you get dressed up to go for an interview. Besides networking, your résumé will probably be the first substantial contact you have with a firm. So to make the grade, your résumé must be professional, accurate, grammatically correct, have an attractive layout, and read well. Don't be cute, garish, or silly with "HIRE ME!" emblazoned at the top of the résumé. Show that you are serious about yourself and about the company. The structure and content—based on your focusing—will go far to show how serious you are.

Most people with more than a decade of experience will have more information than can fit on one page. If you need two pages, use the full length of the second page. Don't type halfway down the second page and stop there, leaving the bottom half blank. You don't need to apologize for a two- or three-page résumé as long as it says what you want it to. But don't belabor a point, either. Remember, the human resources manager who reads your résumé may be frustrated with too much information and put it aside.

After you've revised and edited the résumé to your satisfaction, type it as neatly as possible with the form and layout you want. Remember that your résumé is competing with hundreds of others, so you want to attract the person reading it. Be creative and use plenty of open spaces, headings, and subheadings. If you pack the print too densely on a page, you make it burdensome to read.

Today, with the incredible advances in computers and laser printing, you can file several résumés on a computer diskette and take it to a local office supply store or copier store to print it in minutes. (These stores will often have typewriters or even computer terminals for rent, too.) If you have several types of résumés, copy them in advance. Keep them readily available for distributing when you network as well as for responding quickly to help-wanted ads.

Your copier store has printed thousands of résumés, so they are well-stocked with an assortment of paper colors and textures. Before you select a paper color, check with a few human resource managers and ask them what they look for in a résumé. You want your résumé to stand out, but you don't want it to be cute, either. The typesetters at the copier places have a lot of experience with résumés, so ask them for advice.

The paper stock you select should be conservative, printed with black ink. Whatever you choose, the purpose isn't to draw attention to the résumé itself. You don't want the personnel director to be thinking, "Gee, isn't this slick paper!" or "What a fancy typeface with lots of italics!" You're not advertising the résumé. The résumé is supposed to be advertising you.

Finally, make sure that you keep all receipts from the printer and from any other job hunting expenses—mileage, networking, lunches, phone calls, business cards, and so on. You may be able to deduct them as an expense on your income taxes.

## COVER LETTERS

If you mail the résumé to a company, you will need a cover letter to introduce the résumé to a prospective employer. The cover letter should highlight items in the résumé without duplicating it. The letter must be neat, typed perfectly, with correct grammar and no misspelled words. It should read well and fast, because human resource managers will speed-read the letter on their way to reviewing the résumé. The cover letter should not exceed one page. If it does, you should ask yourself why you need to do that.

When customizing the cover letter, it's best to do some fast networking by calling the human resource manager of the company, if only to ask where to mail the résumé. If you can make such a contact, refer to that connection in the first sentence of the résumé. For example, open the letter with, "This letter is in response to our conversation today about. . . ." If you are responding to an ad from a newspaper or magazine, use that as your hook in the first sentence: "This letter is in response to your ad in. . . ."

After the introduction, concisely tell the reader what job you are applying for. A general or vague "I'm looking for a job" will mean little to a human resources manager who has a specific position to fill.

Then in just a few paragraphs, spell out your experience and qualifications to do that job. Emphasize what you can offer to the prospective employer ("aggressive and creative sales techniques that have led to greater company earnings"). Do not make self-centered statements about what you want to gain from the company ("looking for a high salary and excellent vacation benefits").

Close the letter with a statement like, "I look forward to hearing from you." Be sure that you list your name, address, and phone number on the letter so the prospective employer can contact you.

Of course, you aren't going to wait for that to happen. After a week, call each person you mailed the letter to and ask if he or she received the letter (because mail does get lost). If the letter arrived, ask if they need anything else from you. Finally, ask when you will be hearing from them about an interview.

Unemployment by its very nature distorts your orderly thinking, so you need to be that much more careful about keeping records and doing the necessary follow-up. Keep copies of cover letters and other materials you send to prospective employers. Continue updating your files. Note when you made contacts, what the prospective employers said, what your next step will be, and what you think your chances are.

Finally, be sure to keep your résumé(s) and cover letter(s) current. They aren't static documents. You will find that you will be revising and fine tuning them throughout the course of your job hunt.

## I'M GOOD, AND I'M GOING TO TELL SOMEONE ABOUT ME

If you have spent the necessary time on focusing, writing the résumé and cover letter will be simpler than you imagined. It does involve work—but it's work that will affect your life. So don't hesitate to ask for help. Have your spouse or a friend read over your résumé and make comments. Revise and edit it several times. You should come to the end of the résumé process, read it, and say to yourself, "I'd hire me. I'm that good."

As you gain confidence through focusing and writing the résumé, you already have begun telling others about yourself. It is this networking that is the most effective way of finding a job.

# CHAPTER EIGHTEEN

# The Art of Networking

◆

A dozen adults, ages twenty to sixty, meet at a job support group in a Denver-area church. Their backgrounds appear to have little in common. They range from construction workers and real estate agents to laborers, hospital administrators, journalists, engineers, corporate executives, and those who have no idea what they want to do.

As they share what they want in their job search, they discover they are exchanging information that they would never have found on their own. Names come up. Business cards and phone numbers are exchanged. "Why don't you contact Frank Jones at . . . ?" "I can put you in touch with. . . ."

It may seem like happenstance. But there is a method to this interaction. It's called *networking*. And it's critical to finding new employment.

WHY NETWORK?

Networking is not hanging out with your pals and shooting the breeze about how bad the job market is. That may make you feel good, but only temporarily. It resolves nothing.

Networking is a deliberate, conscious effort to reach as many people as possible who might help you find employment. It marshals what you learned with your focusing and what you wrote in your résumé by targeting your efforts in the marketplace. If you know what you want, you can get other people to help you find it.

Networking is the most effective way of looking for employment.

Denver-area career consultant Neil Duppen said as many as 70 percent of all jobs are found and filled through personal contacts. In contrast, only 5 percent of people find jobs through responses to help-wanted ads. The rest are filled through job-placement agencies, executive-search firms, and position-wanted ads. This isn't to say that you should ignore either newspaper ads or employment agencies. It is to suggest that you focus most of your energy on the methods that work best.

## HOW AND WHERE TO NETWORK
### At Home

Much of your networking will be from your own home via the telephone. This is a great way to get started, especially if your self-esteem is on the ropes. No one can see you or your pain. You can gain confidence dealing with people at your own pace.

But remember that networking over the phone isn't the same as a friendly chat. Your business is to look for work. Here are some ways to act businesslike:

☞ Set aside a desk or work area to be used only for job-hunting.

☞ Don't dress casually. Some people even wear a tie or dress while in their home work area just to put themselves in a proper frame of mind.

☞ Use your best phone etiquette.

☞ Sit up and smile when you talk. (This is not a joke.) When you sit erect and smile (even if you don't feel like it), your voice carries much better—and you enunciate your words more clearly and pleasantly—than when you slouch.

Avoid a shotgun approach to networking, where you blast away at prospects hoping that you'll hit *something*. Instead, target your prospects by selecting a niche—whether a geographical area, a specific industry, or a particular company—and working on it until you have exhausted all possibilities. This strategy will give you much more control over your networking and enable you to track your results more effectively.

The niche you pursue might also be a group of people—for example, clients you have dealt with in the past two years who have given you the best business. If you were able to salvage your client, customer, and source lists from your former job, you have an excellent starting point. If you are a member of a professional society, obtain its membership list. Talk to the people who can get you inside a company without having to go through the regular bureaucratic channels. If the person you contact can't assist you, ask him or her for several other people who may be able to help.

You will get your best results when you do the legwork and phoning yourself. Some employment scams hook unsuspecting job hunters by trying to do their networking for them, and then charging them for it (see chapter 13). However, if you know of a reputable employment agency, you may want to consider enlisting its services. But remember there will be a charge for its services unless companies pay it to find prospective employees. You must evaluate whether you can afford such an agency, especially if your unemployment cash is tight. Finally and most importantly, an employment agency can do little to help you if you haven't done adequate focusing and aren't sure what you want.

Set reasonable goals for yourself, either by numbers of phone calls or by résumés mailed in a day. Don't get discouraged, even if you hear a series of "I don't know of any openings here." Remember that every time you make a contact you let someone, perhaps several people, know who you are and that you're available for work.

## Out on the Street

Then comes the time when you need to get out and pound the pavement. Swallow your pain, put on your best face, and dress the part. It may take some practice to act and speak in an optimistic and constructive manner, but don't give up trying. Anger over what happened to you at your former job or a negative attitude will exude from you like garlic on your breath if you don't check your emotions.

People are much more willing to take a chance on you if you present yourself optimistically, rather than someone who isn't sure of himself or herself. This will come out most obviously by the way you talk. Do you remember being cautioned in the focusing exercises about those voices that may try to tell you to list all your weaknesses, admit all the things you can't do, or dwell on all the things you don't want to do? If you haven't silenced those voices, they will speak for you.

Let's say an eleven-year-old girl clad in green shows up on your doorstep. She has a case of cookie boxes. When you ask what she wants, she responds, "You don't want to buy Girl Scout cookies, do you?" Sort of kills the sale before it's even had a chance, doesn't it? But we do the same thing when we tell a contact, "Well, I worked for Amalgamated Widget, lost my job in a layoff, and now I'm trying to figure out what to do next."

This is where it helps to have thrashed through the process of working on your strengths and job characteristics lists. Once you have done that, you can speak the truth about who you are and what you want. And you can speak it with excitement—ghosts of the past be damned.

Now you know about attitude. Where do you start looking?

You probably already have a network of professionals and clubs with whom you associated in the past. Your friends, of course, can suggest ideas and contacts. Brainstorm with them about networking possibilities. And if you've established even a few local contacts, ask to socialize with them. They have their own watering holes, restaurants, and professional societies, too. Also, don't forget:

- ☞ Family members.
- ☞ Job support groups.
- ☞ Schools and parent-teacher associations.
- ☞ Adult leaders in scouting organizations.
- ☞ Civic groups.
- ☞ Churches and other religious congregations.
- ☞ Political organizations.

Ultimately, the scope of your networking is limited only by your imagination. It may take weeks, months, or even longer. But hang in there. A contact is bound to make the connection for the job you want.

ARMED FOR THE HUNT

Just because you have the greatest intentions to network doesn't mean that you should be out there on your own, starting from scratch. You need several tools, some of which you've already sharpened.

**Know Your Life**

When you network—which will happen virtually every time you meet someone—you need to know what to say. The work you did in the focusing exercises and the résumé writing will become second nature to you. However, you might not be accustomed to talking about yourself, especially in a constructive way. Like many of us, you might even have been conditioned to think that saying something good about yourself is simply prideful bragging. That conditioned mentality will strangle your networking and job hunting.

To counter that conditioning, review your strengths list. Boil down the key points into paragraph-sized chunks. Add specific examples to support those points and accomplishments. Practice reciting those paragraphs in tight sentences using many action verbs. You should feel a sense of excitement as you understand who you are and what you have to offer. Then memorize what you've summarized.

Use every chance you get to rehearse this summary. The best way to go about it is by answering the query, "Tell me about yourself." Imagine yourself in a variety of different social settings: the golf course, parties, community meetings, and so forth. The point of rehearsing what you will say is not to present a "canned" life history. The goal is to make it second nature. You may have only a few minutes—if that—in a social gathering to tell someone about yourself. When you do it concisely, you communicate the information the other person needs to hear. You make a better impression. And you are that much more prepared for the time when you will sit across the desk from a prospective employer in an interview.

### Carry a Résumé

You've spent many hours focusing and then writing your résumé. For all that work, doesn't it make sense to carry a copy with you at all times? You never know who you will meet, or who will be able to put you in touch with someone else. A résumé takes up little room in your briefcase or purse. Many people will fold them up, tuck them in a business envelope with a return address on them, and carry them in their suit jacket. That way, if they meet someone, they can hand the résumé to that person as if it's a piece of business correspondence.

You don't need to get the résumé out and go over each point. You should have your talk down well at that point. The ready résumé is a tangible reminder for the person you've met.

### Buddy, Can You Spare a Card?

Exchanging business cards is a standard ritual when people network. If carrying business cards is important when you do have a job, it's that much more important when you don't.

But if you're unemployed, chances are that you have either your old business cards or none at all. What should you use?

Don't use your old business cards. That's a bad idea for several reasons. First, you don't work for that company anymore, and you don't want to explain why you aren't there. Second, it's nothing but trouble to write your new number or address on the card, especially if you have only a few seconds to pass it along. Third, the old card doesn't represent who you are now.

But having no business card is even worse. Even the veterans of networking while unemployed don't carry résumés with them when they visit the ballpark or attend a social event. Handing off a résumé to a potential contact on a stadium tier while a key play is taking place on the field below will look just plain weird. But you can slip a card to that person as easily as passing a Coke.

There's an easy way to remedy this problem of old cards or no cards. Most office-supply stores and copier places can print personal business cards for a very reasonable price. Depending on the store, the number of lines on the card, and the quality of ink and paper, you can order a stack of a thousand cards for between ten to fifteen dollars. That is a very small price to pay for instant networking. (Be sure to get a receipt for tax time!)

The easiest way to present yourself on a card is simply to print your name, address, and phone number. These office-supply stores display notebooks with samples of typefaces, graphics, and logos you can add. (While you're at it, consider personalized stationery, too.)

Once you design and order your own card, you accomplish important objectives:

☞ You have an instant networking tool that will fit in your wallet, pocket, or purse.

☞ You boost your own self-esteem by proving to yourself that you are equal in this respect to anyone else in the working world.

☞ You show contacts and prospective employers that you take yourself seriously.

Remember that the tools of networking—just like power saws or hammers—are only as good as the expertise of those who wield them. It will take practice to recite your own networking stories and decide when to pass out a résumé or business card. After all, you've probably spent most of your life working, not looking for work. But the more you do it, the more familiar—or even easier—it becomes.

## ON THE THRESHOLD OF A JOB

Then one day, you hit paydirt. The focus, résumé crafting, and networking have paid off. Your résumé made it to the right desk. The contact you made at a professional society calls and says, "I think I've got something for you." You have an interview next week. And you're scared out of your mind. . . .

# CHAPTER NINETEEN

# The Art of Interviewing

---

I t had been five months since Sarah lost her job as an administrative assistant—a job she'd held for nineteen years. She did focus exercises. She crafted an attractive, two-page résumé. She learned how to network through friends, a professional society she discovered, and a job-support group at her church.

After months of looking, the skies opened and showered her with calls for interviews. Unlike many other industries that were imposing hiring freezes, Sarah's industry—health care—was booming. The calls from prospective employers flattered her—and frightened her. Despite her capabilities, she had to learn the ropes of the most critical phase of job hunting: the interview.

Sarah was new to interviewing. She hadn't had to seek work for nearly two decades. She had worked with the same people for years. Answering questions from a stranger who held the power of employment unnerved her.

## PREPARING FOR THE INTERVIEW

Perhaps Sarah's anxiety rings a bell with your own. But you have come too far to mess up now. Ever since you became unemployed, your primary work has been to find a job. In a matter of days or weeks, you will sit across from a stranger who will ask you questions. Your responses and enthusiasm will determine if your unemployment ends there or continues. But even if the thought of an interview scares you, it doesn't mean that you can't think clearly in anticipating your next moves.

## Racing Through Your Thoughts

Interview preparation can be compared to autocross, a car-racing sport gaining popularity. A sports car club creates a course by setting up pylons in a vacant parking lot. Solo drivers race against the clock through the tight, twisting course, rarely shifting out of second gear. The object is to achieve the fastest time while knocking down the fewest pylons. It's pure concentration.

You are about to race through a course, too, attempting to turn in your best performance with the fewest errors. You haven't driven this course before. But you can do what the autocross drivers do: they walk through the course before they get behind the wheel of their car. They mentally rehearse how they will accelerate, anticipate the turns, brake, downshift, turn, and accelerate again.

By getting together with friends who have recently been through the interviewing process, you can get a feel for the employer's interview course. If you can anticipate the turns and the straightaways, you will be that much more comfortable in an interview—despite the fast pace of the course. Many people learn best in crisis situations. When you simulate the climate for the crisis, you will perform better during the real event.

## Practice, Practice, Practice

Career counselor Neil Duppen says that if you've done the focusing, résumé crafting, and networking well, you are already highly prepared for the interview. You have rehearsed the question, "Tell me about yourself." Now you need to know your own answers to these three questions:

1. "*Can* you do the job?"
2. "*Do* you want the job?"
3. "*Will you fit* in the group/firm?"

Of course your answers are important. Just as important, however, is the enthusiasm with which you articulate them. Your face should light up and your posture should show some life as you analyze and respond to them.

Once you have practiced answering these fundamental questions, turn your attention to the standard series of questions that are asked in many interviews. Rehearse your responses to the following inquiries:

☞ "Why do you want this job?"
☞ "Why are you in this career?"
☞ "What are your major strengths?"
☞ "What are your weaknesses?"
☞ "What is the best job you ever had? What is the worst job you ever had? Why?"
☞ "What job are you most proud of?"
☞ "What was your biggest success? What was your biggest failure?"

Practice with friends how you will respond to these questions. You may feel embarrassed, but don't worry about it. Better to have embarrassment now than no job offer later. Most of what you gain from this exercise is confidence that you're doing the right thing.

One of the best ways to tell that you are getting excited and ready for the interview is how much you sit up and talk with your hands. You will find that words alone aren't enough to tell others about yourself. You will gesture, motion, and begin to fill up the room with your own story. Remember your excitement as you approach your first interview, which might not be conducted in person, but rather over the phone.

## THE TELEPHONE INTERVIEW

Increasingly, some companies are using a preliminary telephone interview to save time or avoid shelling out the money to fly a prospective employee to their headquarters. If a company invites you to do a telephone interview, you need to be as sharp as if you walked into its offices. Remember these tips during a telephone interview:

☞ Sit upright at your desk.
☞ Smile and speak clearly.
☞ Have your résumé handy, as well as key points you want to bring up about yourself in case they don't ask.
☞ Have information about the company laid out neatly before you.
☞ Have a list of questions about the company ready.
☞ Take notes, but don't be distracted by your note-taking. You want to respond as naturally as if you were there.

At the end of the interview, ask when they might contact you for an interview in person. Even though an answer isn't a guarantee, they should give you some time frame or deadline. You can then use that as a reference point later when you place a follow-up call at that time—if they haven't called you. You have the right to call them, of course, but don't bug them unnecessarily before the deadline.

## THE PERSONAL INTERVIEW

Neil Duppen cautions that we don't get interviewed very often—that's tough for us. But remember that the interview situation is stressful for both parties. Managers themselves don't interview often, either. Therefore, you have the potential for more control in a personal interview than you might imagine.

### Who's in Charge?

You have control over only one factor in the interview—how you present yourself. How you *perceive* yourself is how you *present* yourself to others. The exercises from focusing will go a long way toward helping you make a good presentation. You, the interviewee, can't rely on the interviewer to draw out your capabilities. You must be prepared to emphasize your own capabilities in the best light, especially if the interviewer fails to bring them up.

At this phase of your job hunting you may be struggling to overcome a fear drubbed into you throughout your unemployment: namely, that you think you're worthless. This is the "Why should anyone want to hire me?" mentality. The problem with it is that you think they're trying to eliminate you. The truth is that *they are trying to find you.*

### Nuts and Bolts

Of course, all the mental preparation will count for little if you fumble the interview in person. That usually happens because of poor planning regarding your appearance and behavior. These basic suggestions are worth repeating:

*Look as sharp as you can*—for men, conservative suit, shirt, and tie; for women, modest and professional-looking dress. Also remember: Shoes polished. Hair neat. Teeth brushed. Fingernails cleaned. No gaudy jewelry. No excessive makeup.

Arrive at least ten to fifteen minutes early. Plan on that margin especially if there is any threat of heavy traffic. The extra time will give you the chance to use the rest room, catch your breath, and mentally walk through the interview one last time.

Remember your manners.

Refuse a drink or food if there is any chance that you might cause a scene by spilling it.

Take notes, but don't let note-taking distract either of you from the conversation.

If you go out to lunch or dinner, don't order food that you eat with your fingers. Stay away from messy foods such as barbecue.

Don't smoke.

Don't drink alcoholic beverages, even if your interviewer does.

Don't apologize for your appearance or any perceived faux pas. This will only draw attention to yourself inappropriately.

If you're ill or depressed, call the company and cancel the interview. Reschedule it for another day.

## What Will They Ask?

By the time you have spent even a few weeks on focusing, writing your résumé, and networking, you will have a good idea of how you will answer the most basic of questions: "Tell me about yourself." Many of the other questions, such as the ones listed previously in this chapter, are variations on that central inquiry. Here are others to consider:

☞ "Why should this company hire you?"
☞ "What are your interests outside work?"
☞ "What would you do in this situation . . . ?"
☞ "What are your goals for the next five years?"

## How to Answer a Question

Answering a question such as "What are your goals?" seems simple enough—except when the answer may affect whether or not you land a job. When you think you're getting shaky in your ability to answer, take a cue from reporters.

When reporters write a hard news story, they use a structure known as the "inverted pyramid." The reporter starts with a broad statement in the first paragraph. That lead sentence concisely includes all the information a reader needs to know: the classic who, what, when, where, why, and how. Then the reporter fleshes out details throughout the rest of the story. Newspapers adopted the inverted pyramid structure so an editor or paste-up person could cut the bottom paragraphs of a story to make it fit on the page without depriving the reader of the crucial information at the top.

Try applying this same technique when you answer questions in the job interview. Make sure you provide the major point first, then add the details. If your conversation is cut short, the interviewer has at least the broad picture of what you're trying to tell him or her.

## Play Your Strengths

Start with what you bring to the job: experience, reputation, education, accomplishments, drive, creativity, or whatever you have refined as your major strengths. Describe what you can offer to the employer. Outline what you can offer to that firm. Let them know that they'll be satisfied and happy that they hired you. Don't bring up personal weaknesses unless they ask you about them. If you must discuss them, don't apologize for them, and give them an upward spin (see below).

*Do not* approach the interview as if you are selecting items from a cafeteria line. Egocentric comments such as, "I want the money," "I want the status," "I want to grow," "I want to expand my horizons," and so forth are tacky at the least. At the most, they will squelch your interviewer's interest in you. These greedy replies reveal childlike attitudes. A company pays you to do a job for them, not to coddle your fantasies of glory.

But you still may feel awkward responding, even though you've rehearsed your answers in front of your friends, in front of the mirror, and behind a truck when you're stuck in traffic. Don't worry: there's a great plan B. Tell your interviewer what others say about you: "My friends say . . . ," or "My coworkers say . . . ," or "My supervisors have said. . . ." This way, you cite an outside opinion that has authority. But if you do invoke others' opinions about yourself, make sure that based on your focusing you know that what they're saying is true—and that you can support their comments with examples.

Depending on your line of work, you have a better ally than even your friends: your accomplishments. Bring examples of reports, documents, publications, objects you've made, or portfolios of designs. These actions really do speak louder than words.

## Answer Questions with an Upward Spin

A conversation is like a game of tennis. One player serves the ball over the net; the other player returns it. If you fail to return the ball, you've lost that point.

When a question is in your court, return it with your best possible swing. This is especially true with "negative" questions such as, "What didn't you like about your former job?" Stay away from negative words, and don't spend the next five minutes badmouthing every supervisor and project you had to put up with in the past two years. Any astute interviewer will take that response as a sign that you won't like his or her company, either. This kind of exchange will torpedo your interview and any chance to work for this prospective employer.

Instead, return this negative question with a straight response followed by an affirmative answer. Say something like, "It was hard to get my supervisor interested in my proposals, but I found that he had high standards and I worked hard to meet them. . . ." This way, you leave the answer on a different and higher plane than the question. The interviewer must then respond to that answer with a like-minded question. As long as you remember that, you can field any question and control the interview.

### Responding to the Ghost

What's the best way to respond when your interviewer asks you why you left your former employer?

Recall how you handled this issue on your résumé. If you were laid off, say so without resorting to bitter or nasty comments. If you were laid off from a large company, and the layoff was well-publicized, you can dispassionately refer to the layoff with something like, "You probably heard that Amalgamated Widget reduced its operations . . . and I was laid off in the transition." Layoffs are not uncommon, so you don't need to belabor the point. Explain what you have learned from the unemployment experience and how you will apply those experiences to your work with the prospective employer.

If you were fired, you will have a much more delicate task. As you know your strengths list, so you should also know the page you wrote explaining why you lost your job. You should be able to recount what happened, briefly and without anger. Compliment those at your former company who helped your career, and keep your mouth shut about those who hurt you. Emphasize how you overcame any deficiency on your part, what you learned, and how those lessons will benefit the prospective employer. After you have explained this situation and turned it toward a constructive direction, be quiet and prepare to answer the next question.

## Keep Your Personal Life to Yourself

You will encounter some sharp people when you go interviewing. They are trying to find out as much about you as they can, even if some of what they want to know, such as the following topics, is forbidden by law:

☞ Sex and age.
☞ Race.
☞ Ethnicity/national origin.
☞ Handicaps and disabilities.
☞ Religion (except when interviewing for religious organizations).
☞ Family matters—marital status, whether or not you have children.
☞ Political views or affiliations.

The answers to these questions have nothing to do with whether you are qualified to do a job. Instead, they give a prospective employer reason to disqualify you for prejudicial reasons unrelated to your capabilities.

You can volunteer this information if you want. But first you should honestly ask yourself: "What is the point of my sharing these personal details? Is this what I want these strangers to know? What does this have to do with working for this firm? How will this hurt me if I tell them?"

Some interviewers are cagey and will try to coax these details out of you. One woman seeking a secretarial position was asked, "How did you happen to move to this area?" She responded, "I was pregnant at the time and followed my ex-husband here fifteen years ago"—and immediately revealed that she was divorced and had a teenager. In this case, she should have said, "I followed my husband here," and left the other personal background out of the interview.

## Questions to Ask the Company

So far, you and the interviewer have been concentrating on those aspects of your experience, abilities, and personality that center on your strengths list. Now comes your turn. Employment is a two-way street, and you have the right and responsibility to know what your prospective employer is about.

Before the interview, do your homework on the company by talking with people who have worked for it and by researching it through its corporate reports and articles on the firm. Using this information and the job characteristics list you made when you did your focusing, consider asking the interviewer the following:

☞ "What are the goals of the company?"
☞ "What is it doing to achieve those goals?"
☞ "What issues create harmony and a sense of purpose?"
☞ "What issues create conflict?"
☞ "Give examples of how people performed their jobs."
☞ "Spell out my duties." (Make sure the interviewer is very specific here, or this could come back to haunt you.)
☞ "What is a day in the life of this company, and in the position for which I'm interviewing, like?"

Close the interview with a polite chat. Make sure the interviewer has a copy of your résumé, a business card, and any other relevant paperwork. Then ask when you will hear from him or her.

Regrettably, the business world often leaves us hanging with "You'll hear back from us." (That shouldn't be surprising since we've done the same thing to others.) Even if they don't get back to you, the door is still open for you to contact them if you ask when you can do so. But regardless of whether or not the interview leads to a follow-up call, mail your interviewer a handwritten thank-you note.

### Follow-Up

If the interviewers don't call you back by the date they set, you have every right to call them. The guidelines are simple, but don't betray your enthusiasm by acting obnoxiously.

☞ Be polite, concise, and direct when you ask them where they are in their decision.
☞ Ask them for their timetable about making a decision.
☞ Ask if you are still a candidate.

Waiting for a response from the company you interviewed and want to work for is not a reason to stop your job hunt cold. During her search for another position in the health care field, Sarah demonstrated to herself and others how much she was in control. She stayed around the house all day on the date when her prospective employer told her he would call, but otherwise she continued with her life as usual. "I ran with my dog. I spent time with my friends, and emotionally pulled away from the interview," she said, adding that she didn't quit looking. "I never stopped my job search. I never let the process stop just because I had something that looked promising."

Sarah's patience and persistence paid off. Five days after she was told she would hear, she mustered her courage and called the firm. They gave her an offer. That in turn raised issues about negotiating the offer.

## WHEN YOU GET AN OFFER

You probably will know no greater feeling of power and self-control during your unemployment than when a prospective employer gives you an offer for a job. Your search of weeks, months, or even years appears to be over. But your unemployment has taught you some lessons in being careful and cautious. And your focusing has helped you discover what you want.

### Negotiating

The feeling of confidence is rich. Indulge in it, but don't let it go to your head. You are the same person you have been. What has changed is that now you have something to negotiate.

Until you have an offer, you have nothing to negotiate. When an employer makes you an offer, you have three options: *accept* it, *reject* it, or *negotiate* it.

Negotiating a job offer doesn't have to be a win/lose situation. It can be a win/win situation. Like so much else in surviving unemployment and looking for work, it boils down to thinking clearly, knowing who you are and what you want. And the touchiest issue probably will be the cash and benefits.

### It's the Money, Honey

Anything to do with money is the most emotional part of an offer. Until you get a specific salary proposal, you can put yourself under unnecessary stress unless you think back on your focusing work.

Remember what you wrote last on the job characteristics list when you did your focusing? It was your minimum salary requirement. As you did your networking, you probably revised that amount. Preferably, you came up with a salary range.

If you get an offer, ask what the salary is. If it is below your range, ask what the employer's policy is about semi-annual or annual increases, bonuses, commissions, and the like. If their response doesn't square with what you had in mind, ask them for some time to consider the offer.

Don't be embarrassed to request a reasonable time to reflect on the offer. Ask the prospective employer when he or she would like your answer. In the meantime, examine the offer, the company, your future coworkers, and your proposed duties. Pay careful attention to your doubts as well as to your excitement. If something the interviewer said or something you saw at the company bothers you, *check it out.* Often your intuitive or "gut" responses are telling you something that may come back to bite you. After all, this is your life you're looking at. Be careful.

Also, check out all other job prospects you have received. You can ride on the confidence you feel of having snared an offer, and use that as leverage with other prospective employers.

But you *will* need to make a decision—to accept the offer, to find a better offer, or to turn down the offer. This is a highly individual decision, which will be influenced not only by the employer making the offer, but also by family and social circumstances. By knowing what you want, you can say a prayer, weigh the other influences, and make a decision. (*Note:* If you are receiving unemployment insurance benefits, you may be required to accept a job offer or risk losing your benefits. Contact your unemployment office or Job Service if you have questions.)

Sarah finally made her decision. She accepted an offer slightly lower than her minimum salary request, but the friendly people she would work for more than made up for the money gap. She even had other offers after the one she took. They were flattering, but she stuck to the commitment she had made.

## WHAT IF YOU DON'T GET AN OFFER?
Even if you survive the gauntlet of résumés, networking, and interviewing, you still may be turned down. Odds are very good, in fact, that you will experience this many times during your unemployment. The competition for work, after all, is stiff.

Being turned down for a job, especially if your presentation was superb, will—like many experiences during unemployment—either weaken you or strengthen you. You know that giving in to despair only hurts you, and in turn hurts your family and friends who are rooting for you.

Whether you are turned down in person, by letter, or by phone, you need to apply the same lessons you learned when you left your former job: act professionally, walk tall, smile, and stay in control of your emotions. You may even want to write a note to your interviewer, thanking her for the time she spent with you, and ask to be kept in mind for any future openings.

You can't take it personally. Even if you have reason to believe that you were turned down because of something as terrible as your former company badmouthing you to prospective employers, you need to behave professionally. (Although if you believe this is happening, you should seriously consider consulting an attorney.)

Many people interviewed for this book have said that they regarded a rejection as a case of them selling something—themselves—to someone who didn't need it. This didn't mean that the product was worthless; it just meant that they weren't a match with the "buyer." They realized that they still had great personal value.

You can't take the rejection lying down, either. If you've been turned down once or many times, fine-tune your focusing and résumé, analyze the market, ask friends for pointers in interviews, and *keep trying*.

As discussed before, and as you're reminded every day, unemployment is hard and it hurts. But I do sincerely believe, as do nearly all the people I've known who have been out of work, that a time *will* come when you do land a job and the darkness passes. And you will then be able to look forward to starting a new life.

## ONCE BURNED, TWICE SHY

As the first day of your new job approaches, you may very well feel queasy. Those three questions you asked yourself earlier in the chapter—"Can you do the job?" "Do you want the job?" and "Will you fit?"—may come back to harass you. You may doubt your ability to perform. You may ask yourself if this is what you really want. And you may wonder if you will get along with your new coworkers.

These doubts may be even stronger if you felt really good when you accepted your former job, only to experience it crashing in flames. In other words, you don't want to go through all that disappointment—and the subsequent unemployment—again.

These jitters are understandable. They've probably been nurtured by months of unemployment, reinforced by countless rejections from other companies, and crystallized by a fractured self-esteem. If you've had to move and uproot your family, the pressures mount even more. You may perceive that those who depend on you or supported you are laying incredible expectations on you. And you wonder if you will ever be able to recover your financial losses with what may be a lower salary.

*Relax.* Your new company hired you because it wanted you. It wanted you because *you* knew what you wanted after thinking through your strengths and desires. You forged those job convictions while growing tough through unemployment. You found that those who depend on you and love you are rooting hard for your success.

The doubts about your abilities or your compatibility with coworkers will fade, and probably fade fast. You will find that you can do the job, and most likely that it's better than you thought. The smiles from your new colleagues will melt your fears, and maybe even your heart. You'll meet new people, have a new purpose—and earn a new paycheck.

Welcome to your new life.

## IT'S NOT OVER TILL IT'S OVER—AND IT'S NEVER OVER

Finding a job you want is a tremendous relief that exceeds even the agony you endured in the wasteland of unemployment. You survived the trial and the trials. But the lessons haven't ended. They will never end as long as you are part of the working world.

You can't prevent another layoff or firing. As the world economy grows more interdependent and competitive, it's very possible that you will lose your job again. Now you need to prepare for the future by developing strategies that you will need to survive the next possible period of unemployment.

# CHAPTER TWENTY

# When You Are Employed Again

❖

More than likely, you will work again, whether with another company or by striking out on your own. You'll start a new life, gain a new group of friends and colleagues, maybe even move to a new city or state. It's wonderful to be wanted, and it's wonderful to contribute to a company's growth.

You have so much to look forward to. But you also have so much you'd like to forget. You should do the former, but you should change your mind about the latter.

It's easy to want to forget about your time of unemployment, just as you want to forget about any difficult period of life. However, you've learned some valuable lessons about yourself, your personal relationships, and your finances. Don't forget them. These lessons will mean that much more if you are still unemployed as you read this.

You've learned that unemployment can happen to anyone. And you know that it could happen again. But the next time around, you can be better prepared with your finances, family circumstances, and attitudes.

These attitudes include more than just watching your step and thinking ahead—important as those are. We all need to forge a new self-reliance in order to adapt to the technological and social changes on the horizon. But this self-reliance needs to be tempered with compassion so that it does not become simply a self-seeking way of protecting personal interests. We're all on this journey through life together. You can do a favor to those still out of work by showing the kind of empathy possible only from those who have struggled through such a trial. You will be stronger for these experiences, and that strength can help others as well as yourself.

## APPLYING THE LESSONS YOU'VE LEARNED

So now you're working again. It feels great, doesn't it? You're part of a team. You have a purpose, goals, and projects to complete. As we explored in the self-esteem chapter, that's a natural part of who we are: we want to create. And, of course, there's that paycheck. No more worries about whether you'll be able to pay the mortgage or put dinner on the table.

The memories of those last few terrible hours or days at your former employer's have dimmed with time. So have the memories of standing in the unemployment line, thrashing out a budget, and riding out the stresses of your family's life.

But you've changed, perhaps in some of the same ways as the individuals and families represented in the book. Steve and Barb (chapter 10) strengthened their relationship with each other and grew closer to their children. Steve, in particular, gained compassion. Before his job loss, he callously dismissed the unemployed as people who got what they deserved. Now he leads prayer and support groups for the unemployed.

Gene and Teresa (chapter 10) also experienced growth in family intimacy. But their unemployment did something else as well: it honed an attitude of self-reliance. "I'll never be the same type of employee again," Gene said. "I think I won't take anything for granted anymore. I appreciate what companies do for you, but now I recognize it's a business. In the end you have to make yourself valuable and keep your eyes open. Don't get complacent and float along."

Can you ever just float along again? Can you be complacent when you recall the nights you lay in bed, staring at the ceiling and wondering if any of the firms you'd contacted in the past month would ever call? Can you casually dismiss the frightened looks in the eyes of your spouse and children when your own anxiety spilled over into harsh words? Can you ever really forget what it felt like to stand in the unemployment line, and then six months later hold your last benefits check, wondering, *What's next?*

This isn't supposed to be an exercise in feeling bad. It's an exercise in real life—using memories to spur you to action in finances and other personal behavior.

## Pent-up Demand

"Now that I've got a job, I'm going to buy. . . ."

Not so fast. Before you lustfully eye that credit card, fantasizing what you will do with it at the mall, consider this: You are experiencing a common reaction to a dry spell in your personal finances, known as "pent-up demand." You probably were hankering for a few things before you or your spouse lost a job. In the meantime, you watched your clothes take a shine. You heard your music collection retreat from new hits to old classics. Now you want to get even.

But the big problem of getting even is that the bully you want to beat up is stronger than you. Yielding to your pent-up demand may put you in serious debt. This is especially true if you've been out of work for a year or more, you need to move, and you take a lower paying job than you had before. If you will stop and think, you will find you can do much better with your finances than blitzing the mall.

## Assessing Your Finances, Part Two

You learned some valuable lessons about money during your unemployment. You found that you really *could* live on less—perhaps a lot less—than you ever imagined. Why not apply that discipline to your finances? In the long run, it will make you feel much better than the rush from a shopping spree.

Remember that personal finance isn't a problem of not having enough money. It's an issue of thinking clearly about who you are, what you make, what and how you spend, and what you save. As financial planners are fond of saying, "It isn't what you make, it's what you keep."

A variety of excellent books and resources are available to help you with financial planning—from monthly budgets to savings, insurance, investments, and retirement. Also, consider contacting your local Consumer Credit Counseling Service and attending a money control workshop. Find something that works for you, and *stick with it*. Remember that your checkbook is the greatest evidence of what you really believe about yourself, your family, and your God.

You might also benefit from evaluating these other areas of personal finance in the immediate future:

*Retreat from "charge!"* When you were out of work, you probably broke some bad habits about credit card debt. So instead of maxing out that magic plastic now that you're working, why not discipline yourself to pay off your consumer debt? Take a small percentage of your income, and every month pay down those credit cards. Keep doing this, and you will feel a power that you haven't known for quite a while. Instead of smiling briefly over that new toy you bought, learn what it is to sense the inner peace and strength that you don't owe anyone anything— except a debt of love.

*A net worth analysis.* Take a sober inventory of your assets, your investments, your debts, and your long-range financial goals. Many people work for years without ever knowing how rich—or how poor—they really are.

*Rainy days and monsoons.* Before you lost your job, you heard the line about "saving for a rainy day." Now you know that you need to save for monsoon seasons. Financial planners maintain that every working person should have at least three months' to six months' cash saved for such an emergency. Families with children should consider deeper pockets than this. If unemployment strikes again, you will feel powerful and confident with such a cash reserve.

*Reduce the stress in your life.* They were all too infrequent during unemployment, but you learned how to throw little celebrations for yourself when you experienced little blessings. You also learned the value of prayer, laughter, exercise, and a steady routine. All these elements helped fight the stress that knocked you down and immobilized you. Now that you are working again, weave these good habits into your daily life.

*The importance of your family and close friends.* Your unemployment put great stress on your family or close relationships, perhaps more than you realized. If you grew closer together, remember what crises you overcame and think how you can apply those lessons for continued growth. However, just because your unemployment is over doesn't mean that all wounds are healed. Don't hesitate to seek counseling from friends or professionals if relationships between you and your spouse—or you and your children—are still strained.

*The importance of your community.* Through your networking, you found just how much is available—or unavailable—to those who are out of work. You necessarily cut back on your charitable giving. You can resume that now. Better still, volunteer with a local social services agency. Start a job-support group. Baby-sit for parents who are out looking for work. Unemployment is a fact of life for somebody at any given time, and you've learned valuable lessons to impart to them.

*The importance of being prepared.* Even if you take action on all these suggestions, however, it will mean little if you forget the biggest unemployment lesson of all: *It can happen again.* If you forget that, you'll forget the other lessons, too. You can't control the larger forces going on in technology or the global economy. But you certainly can watch for them and plan accordingly.

KEEPING THE BIG PICTURE IN FOCUS
No one can predict whether future ebbs and flows of recession and growth will mean greater upheavals in our personal lives through unemployment. But a few things are certain. The business cycle is inevitable. And political rhetoric aside, we *do* live in a new world order. This doesn't mean that we all live on one big happy planet. But we're never going back to the insulated national economies to which we once pledged allegiance.

The economies of the world are becoming increasingly integrated, said Jon Talton, a business columnist who writes about political economy for Denver's *Rocky Mountain News*. Politicians and governments are rapidly losing their ability to control a national economy. Increasingly, it's as easy to buy goods and services across national borders as it is to buy them across the street.

This revolutionary change has profound implications for workers. Their skills—whether blue-collar or white-collar—won't be measured by company, community, or national standards, Jon said. Workers will compete with the skills of other workers around the world. Yet even as traditional patterns in corporations, business, and labor unions grow obsolete, new patterns are emerging. And we are more able to act on our own.

That new competition, and those new abilities, have been fired by the information revolution—to a much greater extent than occurred in previous agricultural and industrial revolutions. Technology has empowered people in ways unimaginable a generation—not to mention a century—ago. For example, the power of a notebook computer that can fit in a briefcase could not have fit in a *house* in 1960. We have only barely begun to see the impact of the personal computer and other emerging technologies.

Jon explained that emerging technology means more than amazing gizmos. The new technology is also gutting the institutions we once put so much stock in. Today, people can do far more work out of their homes than people a generation ago could do by working overtime in an office, or people two generations ago could do by working in a factory. To get business done, we don't need big companies or big institutions. To work or shop, we don't need to live in or near an urban corporate, retail, or industrial center.

We have more options, power, and flexibility than our parents did. Our children will have more options than we do. We have more ways to succeed. And we have more ways to fail.

Change has always meant hardship, even as it has often brought greater freedom and better products. Early this century, buggy manufacturers were laying off workers and going out of business. But Henry Ford was hiring workers to make his Model T cars at the astonishingly high rate of five dollars a day. It was hard for workers then, as it is hard for most of us now. Many technological changes bring dislocation and pain—but many bring long-term benefits as well.

We can't hold back these changes, although we can hope to guide the use of technology for peaceful and constructive purposes. We can't prevent all of the risks, although we can eliminate some of them. We can't stop the global changes from affecting us, but we can control our own responses by training ourselves to become self-empowered.

## THE ROAD TO SELF-EMPOWERMENT

Unemployment taught you fast and hard that you need to take control of your life. You didn't need to listen to a motivational speaker or read a book to tell you that you needed to find work. You knew that if you didn't get out of bed, get dressed for the day, and take care of business, it wouldn't happen.

It all seemed so frantic and crazy at first. But over time, you found that you could do jobs, albeit temporary ones, that you never thought you could—or would—do otherwise. Circumstances forced you into those patterns of behavior.

The next time around, circumstances and your reactions to them can be different. This will require self-empowerment, self-discipline, and flexibility. You can't predict which new technological, political, or social developments will touch your life in the next decade. But you know that change is inevitable, and you can get ready for it.

Instead of ignoring the changes until after they've washed over you, you can train yourself to roll with them, if not ride their waves. In fact, the more you learn, the better prepared you will be for finding a job you want, rather than clinging to one you don't like that supports the rusting idol of "job security." That kind of job isn't long for the contemporary workplace, anyway.

These are just a few suggestions to get you—and your children, too—started as a self-empowered, flexible person who anticipates the future:

☞ Turn off the television.

☞ Read good books and good journals.

☞ Find some people with whom you can have intelligent conversations.

☞ Learn a foreign language.

☞ Learn to track business and marketplace trends.

☞ Vacation in a foreign culture.

☞ Transform a hobby into a small business.

☞ Learn to use a computer and a variety of software programs.

☞ Volunteer at a place where you learn something new about people.

Now that you're employed again, you may be tempted by comments from friends, family, or new coworkers to fall back on the soothing presumption, "Everything's all right now, so don't worry about it." Thinking about another layoff or firing is just dwelling on the negative past, they say, and hey, shouldn't we be having fun?

I've got nothing against fun. But I'm definitely against foolishly ignoring the experiences of the past months by thinking that unemployment may not happen again—and that I don't have to prepare for it.

INDEPENDENCE, COMPASSION, AND COMMUNITY

A number of recent political and technological changes demonstrate that things are different in our generation. On one hand, we have seen the collapse of international communism and the rise of centuries-old ethnic conflicts. On the other hand, we are participating in an unprecedented revolution in technology, information, and a global economy. We see cooperation that springs from the ground up: People from every country can talk to each other across national borders with electronic gadgets—never mind what their politicians forbid them to do.

People are now much more independent, assertive, self-reliant, and free. Yet as the cooperation takes hold, old hatreds and fears come alive, too. We negatively label foreigners, blaming them for taking our jobs. Those we can't blame, we ignore: from tribal children starving for food in the Horn of Africa to urban children starving for justice in Los Angeles.

Those of us who have felt the sting of unemployment have tasted what it's like for those who—until recently—lived on the other side of the television screen. We've grown through struggle. We've disciplined ourselves to think clearly. We've learned gratitude for those who have helped us, and we want to repay the kindness.

We hope that as we return to the working world, we will resurrect the work ethic of our parents that produced so much for their children—without the damaging side of that work ethic, which stigmatized the unemployed. Hard work is a virtue. Creativity is what we were made for. But hard work and creativity don't preclude decency. Some corporations are changing to recognize and honor the labor, suggestions, and ideas of all their employees, not just those in the executive suites. Regrettably, many are not changing.

More corporations need to learn to treat their employees better, not just because it's good for the bottom line—which it is—but because it is the just and moral thing to do. Too often, the egos of insecure people in management positions run unchecked through offices and shops like bullies on the playground. Let's hope that as more managers are laid off, experience unemployment, and return to work, they can turn their pain into compassion for those who work for them.

Managers, like the rest of us, are learning how fragile and fleeting security really is. Few institutions can claim to offer security: not corporations, not unions, not governments, not political systems.

Instead, the security that we've found is much closer to home, whether it's our family, a local job-support group, shared tips on who's hiring, or shared soup at a community shelter. This is security from the ground upward and the heart outward. We can barely control what happens in our state or national capitals—whether Washington, Ottawa, Tokyo, or Moscow. Political action can shape government policy on labor and employment, but it can rarely control what happens to XYZ Corporation in the center of downtown.

So it's up to us. We have learned that we can control—that we must control—what happens in our personal and family lives if we are to survive unemployment.

Now that we're working again, it's the responsibility of those of us who have endured unemployment—especially those who would have sworn only a few years ago, "It will never happen to me"—to apply these lessons of finances, family, self-esteem, wariness, resourcefulness, and community. It's not at all unreasonable to expect that we will lose a job again. But the next time around—and the next time around after that—we can hope that surviving unemployment will be that much more bearable, and that our capability for giving love will be that much deeper.

Solution to the puzzle on page 168.

## APPENDIX A:
## SAMPLE LETTER TO A CREDITOR

(Date)

Creditor
ABC Credit, Inc.
123 Main Street
Anycity, USA 00000

Dear Creditor:

My name is _____ and my credit account number
is _____. I am temporarily unemployed because
of a layoff from _____ (or list other reason). I have
analyzed my current financial situation with the help of (Consumer Credit
Counseling Service or other agency) and have worked out an emergency
budgeting and spending plan.

I need to provide basic living expenses for myself and my family, plus make
credit payments. I am asking each of my creditors to accept reduced payments until the situation is resolved and I have returned to work.

Your cooperation will help my situation greatly. I will be making reduced
monthly payments of $_____ instead of $_____
until this difficult time is over.

Please be assured that I will resume normal payments as soon as I find work.
I will notify you if my situation changes.

Thank you for your understanding and cooperation.

Sincerely,

(Signature)

Name
Address
Phone number
Credit account number

*(Courtesy of Consumer Credit Counseling Service of Southern Colorado.)*

# APPENDIX B:
## OTHER RESOURCES FOR SURVIVING UNEMPLOYMENT

A trip to any bookstore or library will unearth a treasure trove of books on aspects of financial planning, job hunting, résumé writing, and so forth. You can also get help from a variety of publications and organizations. To mine these resources effectively, you need to know in advance what kind of specific assistance you most need.

To give you a head start, the following list highlights a few recommended resources for guiding you through the journey of unemployment. Remember, however, that your finances are tight. Buying books or subscribing to newsletters may not be a responsible decision. You can always check your local library for these resources. If you know other jobless friends, you may want to pool your cash or other resources, buy books and/or subscriptions, and then share them.

NEWSLETTERS

*Bottom Line/Personal*. A semimonthly newsletter with the stated purpose, "To help those who are very busy with their careers handle their personal lives more effectively." The content covers just about everything: parenting, investing, health, emotions, consumer news, and more. It culls information from a wide variety of sources, but you pay a price for it—$49 per year. You may not be as busy as many of its readers, but it's still worthwhile. Check your local library or write:

> Bottom Line/Personal
> Boardroom Reports, Inc.
> 330 W. 42 St.
> New York, NY 10036

*Rotten Times*. A monthly newsletter targeted specifically to the jobless, featuring tips on coping with daily life and the job search. It also offers information on the broader picture of unemployment. For information and subscriptions, write:

> Rotten Times
> P.O. Box 1440
> Williamsburg, VA 23187

*The Tightwad Gazette*. The authoritative newsletter on how to do a lot more for a lot less, by Yankees who really know what thrift is all about. For information and subscriptions, write:

> The Tightwad Gazette
> R.R. 1
> Box 3570
> Leeds, ME 04263-9710

BOOKS

*Career Shock: How to Make Your Own Choices — and Stay in Control of Your Career*. A good, short volume on how to take control of your life when you feel as if your life is spinning out of orbit. Author James C. Cotham, III, is Graduate Professor of Management Strategy and Policy at the Jack C. Massey Graduate School of Business (Nashville, Tennessee). Published in 1988, this small book is now in paperback for under $5. If you can't find it, write:

Berkley Books
The Berkley Publishing Group
200 Madison Avenue
New York, NY 10016

***Do What You Love, The Money Will Follow***. This best-selling book by psychologist Marsha Sinetar has guided thousands to choose their "Right Livelihood," as she calls it. It is not about wishing yourself a job and waking up with a bundle of cash, but rather how to listen to your deepest longings, refine your self-esteem, and become personally successful. Check the career section of your bookstore or library, or write:

Dell Publishing
Bantam Doubleday Dell Publishing Group, Inc.
666 Fifth Ave.
New York, NY 10103

***Making the Most of Your Money: Smart Ways to Create Wealth and Plan Your Finances in the '90s***. Syndicated columnist Jane Bryant Quinn leaves no stone unturned in this book on personal financial management. Whether she's writing about marriage, insurance, investing, or retirement, it's well-organized and witty (an important benefit in the tedious world of managing your cash). If you can't find it at your library or bookstore, write:

Simon & Shuster
Simon & Shuster Building
Rockefeller Center
1230 Avenue of the Americas
New York, NY 10020

***Resumes That Knock 'em Dead***. Author Martin John Yate's book is regarded as one of the best in the glutted field of résumé-writing resources. Yate guides the reader through the technical and sometimes maddening process of crafting a résumé and a cover letter, and then provides advice on how to use them. Yate, also the author of *Knock 'em Dead with Great Answers to Tough Interview Questions,* offers examples of more than one hundred successful résumés in as many different fields. Although your unemployment dollars are tight, they're not so tight that you can't afford this. See your local bookstore, library, or write:

Bob Adams, Inc.
260 Center Street
Holbrook, MA 02343

***What Are You Worth?*** Edward M. Hallowell, M.D., and William J. Grace, Jr., have written a straightforward and engaging study to help you define your psychological orientation regarding money and then guide you to financial well-being. The authors—a psychiatrist and a stockbroker—help you define the emotional ways you regard money. Then they identify your "money style," such as "The Jock," "The Optimist," "The Pessimist," "The Worrier," and so forth. Check your library or write:

Weidenfeld & Nicolson, New York
A Division of Wheatland Corporation

841 Broadway
New York, NY 10003-4793

***What Color Is Your Parachute?: A Practical Manual for Job-Hunters & Career-Changers***. This classic book is still the ultimate resource on finding yourself as you find work. For more than two decades, Richard Nelson Bolles has annually revised this probing, reflective, spiritual, and often downright fun (lots of cartoons, graphics, and Victorian woodcuts) journey through career-land. More than four million copies have been sold. It's widely available at bookstores and libraries, as are other helpful books for the job hunter by Ten Speed Press. If you can't find it, write:

Ten Speed Press
P.O. Box 7123
Berkeley, CA 94707

OTHER RESOURCES

***The AFL-CIO***. No book on working, or slogging through the land of unemployment to get back to work, would be complete without mentioning the organization and its member trade unions, which have been the social and legal support for millions of workers. The AFL-CIO can be found in every state, as can its programs. Most state AFL-CIOs and their trades training directors run Job Training Partnership Act programs for dislocated workers in conjunction with the federal government. For more information, call your state's office of the AFL-CIO.

***The Consumer Information Catalog***. A *very* slim but useful resource for access to consumer information. Published by the U.S. General Service Administration, it offers more than two hundred government booklets and pamphlets on everything from money, health, and housing to employment, education, and small businesses. The booklets and pamphlets range in price from free to a few dollars. For a copy of the catalog, write:

Consumer Information Catalog
Consumer Information Center—2B
P.O. Box 100
Pueblo, CO 81002

***National Business Employment Weekly***. Published by Dow Jones & Company, Inc., this paper rightly bills itself as "The Nation's Premier Job-Search Publication Since 1981." It combines help-wanted ads from all regional editions of *The Wall Street Journal*, and contains articles on job-hunting, networking, interviewing, and financial advice. You can find it at your local newsstand, bookstore, or library or write:

National Business Employment Weekly
c/o *The Wall Street Journal*
420 Lexington Ave.
New York, NY 10170

You also may call (800)JOB-HUNT/(800)562-4868, or (212)808-6791.

# INDEX

# AUTHOR

Tom Morton survived unemployment for seventeen months. He is an award-winning reporter with a decade of experience in religion, investigative, and environmental journalism. He has written for the *Beaumont (Texas) Enterprise,* the *Colorado Springs (Colorado) Gazette Telegraph,* and the *Casper (Wyoming) Star-Tribune,* as well as other newspapers, magazines, and news services. He graduated from Miami University in Oxford, Ohio, and Gordon-Conwell Theological Seminary in South Hamilton, Massachusetts. He also has taught sociology of religion at the University of Colorado at Colorado Springs.